MW00627861

CATCH ME UP

LESSONS IN ENTREPRENEURSHIP OVER 50

BY
WILLIAM SHATNER

WITH
NILS PARKER

Paperback - ISBN 978-0-9961923-0-9

Hard Cover - ISBN 978-0-9961923-1-6

Special Edition Hard Cover - ISBN 978-0-9961923-2-3

Printed in the United States of America.

Bang Printing, 3323 Oak Street, Brainerd, MN 56401.

Http://www.bangprinting.com.

First Printing, 2015

TABLE OF CONTENTS

INTRODUCTION

If you're over 50 years old and reading this right now, one of two things has probably already happened to you: either the new economy has risen up and bitten you in the ass or you've seen it happen to someone you care about and you realize you're unprepared for when it happens to you. Whichever camp you fall into, you're not alone. In the wake of the 2007-08 financial crisis and the "Great Recession" that followed, similar stories have been playing out across the country. **As if our over-50 asses didn't have enough problems!**

Workers—both blue and white collar—have seen their 401Ks, IRAs and money market funds decimated. At the same time, they watched as large multinational companies streamlined operations, trimming the fat (translation: their jobs) in order to stay profitable. And profitable they stayed, at record levels in fact. The Dow bounced back and rocketed past the **17,000 mark.** The S&P 500 took it on the chin but has since vaulted over 2000. **But it seems the only people benefitting are the bankers and the ladies who strip for them. I don't know about you, but my years of looking good in a g-string are long gone.**

What haven't bounced back are the jobs. That's the dirty little secret of this recovery. Corporations are making record profits and the stock market indexes are hitting record highs because big business has realized they can be just as productive with half the people. All those jobs that companies had to cut when things went south in 2007-08? They don't need them anymore. They may have never needed them if you were to ask some CEOs, and this downturn was their chance to trim that fat. **(And If you don't like being called 'fat,' then for God's sake stay out of show business!)**

There's a new book out called "Choose Yourself", by an ex-hedge fund manager and entrepreneur named James Altucher, which first made this new reality totally clear for me. I knew something was up before I read it, there was something fishy about this new environment in which we found ourselves, I just couldn't put my finger on it. Too many of my fans were still struggling. Too many of my friends, and their friends and families, were worried not just about making it through retirement (what if the money that was left dried up too fast?) but even making it to retirement (would they ever be able to retire now?). This passage from "Choose Yourself" really opened my eyes:

I recently visited an investor who manages more than a trillion dollars. You might think a trillion dollars sounds impossible. I did. But there's a lot more money out there than people let on. It's squirreled away by families who have been hoarding and investing and reinvesting for hundreds of years. And this trillion dollars I speak of belonged to just one family.

We were high up in the vertical city of New York. His entire office was surrounded by glass windows. He brought me over to one of them. "What do you see?" he said.

I don't know, I thought. Buildings.

"Empty floors!" he said. "Look at that one. Some bank. All empty." He pointed at another building. His fingers scraping across his window like...I don't know...whatever a spider uses to weave its web. "And that one: an ad agency or a law firm or an accounting firm. Look at all the empty desks. They used to be full, with full-time employees. Now they're empty and they will never fill up again."

I spoke with several CEOs around that time and asked them point-blank, "Did you fire people simply because this was a good excuse to get rid of the people who were no longer useful?"

Universally, the response was a nervous laugh and a "Yeah, I guess that's right!" And because of the constant economic uncertainty, they told me, they are never going to hire those people again.

Yeah... they're nervous.

That is the world, the new economy, we live in today; a world of empty floors. Countless articles have been written about the plight of the poor, the undereducated, the lower middle class, veterans, all of whom were the ones kicked out of those now-vacant office suites and are having a hell of a time getting back in. Their circumstances are very real and certainly very difficult. One group you haven't heard much about in this discussion, however, is yourselves.

At, or nearing retirement age, Americans over 50 years old face a unique yet equally difficult set of challenges in the new economy. You have more experience, which is good, but your average salary demands are higher, which is bad. You don't make a lot of mistakes, which is good, but you move a little slower than the younger candidates who will work for 60% of what you're asking, which is bad. You have a great work ethic and take pride in your work, which is good, but you aren't as comfortable with the rapidly changing technology landscape as the Millennials, which is bad. **Finally — let's end on a positive — you can name all the members of Led Zeppelin, which is good.**

This puts you in a tough spot in the job market. Assuming, of course, that you're looking for a "job."

In the rest of the chapter, titled "Permanently Temporary", Altucher goes on to describe the new economy. The circumstances—the conditions on the ground—are nothing you haven't already heard, read, seen or felt. But, he says, as a worker, the new economy has given you two choices: permanent temporary employment or creative entrepreneurship.

You don't have to throw yourself into the job market. You can create your own market. You don't have to knock on every door in town hoping that someone will hire you. **You can hire yourself.**

And what's more, with greater experience, stronger networks, better financial resources and credit histories, Americans over 50—you brilliant silver foxes, you!—are uniquely situated to take fullest advantage of the entrepreneurial opportunities created by the tectonic shifts of the new economy. Not only can you leap into the next phase of your lives, but you can secure your financial future in the process.

Now you're probably wondering what the hell William Shatner is doing writing this book. You're probably thinking: *William Shatner is rich and famous and devilishly handsome* (and you'd be right, by the way), *he has no idea what I'm dealing with!*

Well, that's where you'd be wrong. I am a professional actor. I have been permanently temporarily employed my entire life. According to the entertainment website IMDB.com, since 1951, I have had more than 400 different roles in television and film (not including talk show guest appearances). That means in 60+ years in my profession I've had 400+ jobs. And even more frightening, at least looking back on it from my perspective, that means I was unemployed hundreds of times too. **If they gave me a medal for each time I was jobless, I wouldn't be able to stand up.**

And I'm not alone. Professional actors spend most of their careers unemployed. We are out of work all the time. Every time we finish a show--be it a television segment, a movie, stage production, commercial, voiceover gig, pretty much anything actors do to keep alive—we're out of a job. So you don't have to tell me about job hunting or the anguish of being unemployed. I know the bitter taste of not working. I know the stomach clenching feeling of wondering where your next dollar is coming from or how you will keep a roof over your head or how you will support everyone else who depends on you to make enough money to stay alive.

I have been there. When I was a kid, I was there. When I was a young man, I was there. Even as a middle-aged man, I was there. And when I got older than middle aged, somewhere between stiff and decrepit, I was still there.

It was around this time, in the doldrums of the mid-1990s after the long run of Star Trek movies that covered the entire 1980s really, that I got tired of being there. I searched and searched for a way out until finally I found my answer one morning. It was staring back at me in the mirror. I was my own way out. **Also, I needed a shave, but you get the picture.**

I'd been in the business for 50 years at that point. I had some money. I had a ton of experience. I knew the tricks to exploit and the pitfalls to avoid. I didn't need studio or network executives to sign off on whether I was a good fit for this or that project—though I would never turn down their offers if the money was right; I'm not crazy! I realized that if I wanted to do something—a commercial, a book, an album, a horse show—I could just go do it myself. I could make it happen. I didn't just have to be William Shatner, the actor. I could be William Shatner, LLC. William Shatner Incorporated. William Shatner™. **William Shatner.com. (Go ahead – check it out!).**

Don't misunderstand, in many ways, even if it doesn't show on my balance sheet, I am still there in my mind, in my soul. I am there every time I finish something and I think to myself, I wonder what's

** My IMD profile page: http://www.imdb.com/name/nm0000638/*

next? I wonder if there will even be a next. I start thinking about whether I can physically survive another tour, a long movie shoot, or a 24-hour flight to some distant location. These are heady questions about life and career and mortality. What has pulled me back from that pit of anguish and that stomach clenching feeling has been the ability to hire myself.

It's an ability we all have, especially those of us over 50 years old. That's why this book is for you. It will help you appreciate those unique skills you've developed over the years. It will help you identify those areas where you might need to get stronger. And most importantly, it will teach you how to ride this wave of entrepreneurial spirit by identifying specific ways you can **HIRE YOURSELF.**

So if I may, I will conclude by bastardizing my cherished late friend Leonard Nimoy's most famous line:

Live longer and prosper!

William Shatner

CHAPTER ONE

ON THE WRONG SIDE OF RIGHT-SIZING: A PATHWAY TO CONSULTING

MICHAEL GRATTOLA

CONSULTANT

Full Shatner Interview: CatchMeUp.com/Michael

Upper Saddle River is one of those affluent towns in the northern part of New Jersey where, for years, people have aspired to live. **It's like heaven, if heaven were on Rte. 17 in Bergen County.** When I first came to Broadway in the 1950s, many of the husbands and wives who came to the theater on a Friday or Saturday night came in from towns just like Upper Saddle River. Today, its streets are lined with large, recently built single-family homes. Volvo station wagons and German SUVs dot the driveways. Kids walk around tethered to iPhones and iPads on their way to soccer or lacrosse practice. All of these things—these symbols of having made it, of the American Dream—were purchased by the children of the husbands and wives who came to see a Broadway show all those years ago. They are the men and women who commute across the Hudson River into Manhattan every day for high-powered, high-paying jobs in high-status, high-pressure companies. **And if they ride home in the bar car now and then, who can blame them? They earned it.**

In 2009, Michael Grottola was one of these people: an executive consulting giant KPMG. He would turn 65 that year with two teenage daughters preparing to go to college and a big house with an even bigger mortgage. By his own admission, executive management was not where Grottola ever thought he would end up. He was an electrical engineer by training, having spent most of his early professional years around software and technology. His first job out of college was with a premises protection company in New York City that designed the first automated computer monitoring system in the world and subsequently stiffed him on a raise. From there he went to work for Lockheed Missiles and Space. These were not the beginnings of any path to management or consulting that I'd ever heard of, especially in the early 1970s when this was all taking place for Michael. Then again, what do I know? I was just an actor back then. *Star Trek* had already been canceled and I was bouncing from guest role to guest role on a bunch of TV shows no one remembers. When you think about it, both our fates were rather uncertain.

Fortunately for Michael, the entrepreneurial spirit that was baked into his DNA along with a little luck and great timing led him into small business and self-employment. A little more than a year into his tenure at Lockheed, the premises protection company in New York came calling, this time with their tail between their legs.

"No, no, no. Come back!" Michael recounted the conversation to me. "We want you here."

It always feels great to be wanted. It feels even better when two people want you and one of them knows they made a huge mistake letting you go the first time. A smart man, even in his mid-20s, Michael knew he had the leverage.

"At the time, I thought to myself, you know what would be great? If I had my own business. I could deal with my expenses, work with other companies. I wouldn't have to sit at a desk. I just wanted to be free."

Who doesn't? So Michael made them an offer.

"Okay, I'll come back, but you have to put me on retainer...for double my old salary. They said yes. That's how it started. I essentially played at having a business because I had one customer. And that customer called me back. But then I got another customer, and another customer."

Like they say, "Fake it till you make it." Michael Grottola, at 25 years old, eased himself into his own business by identifying an opportunity, seizing it, and then working his butt off.

"I gave them everything I had," he recalled to me, almost wistfully. "I'd work day and night. I was willing to work around the clock. I ran into situations where I had no idea how I was ever going to do this. And somehow, by not quitting, by asking for help from the right people, by getting a huge amount of assistance, I figured it out."

He built a successful small business on this philosophy and on the back of this kind of work ethic. For Michael, there was no problem too big or client too small. One time, in the mid-'90s, for instance, he and his team spent an entire weekend—at their own expense—at a client's office to address a daunting problem they just could not seem to solve. **It was Saturday Night Fever, but with less disco and more Sysco.**

"The software we installed on this client's computers kept failing and failing. The problem was so bad, the computers actually started failing. So we're into the software and we're into the hardware. We can't figure it out. It's getting late and I said to one of the guys that worked for me, 'We don't need those lights on down there. Let's save electricity. Shut the lights off.' As soon as he shut the lights off, the computer went down. I said, 'Do that again!' Rebooted everything, shut the lights off, computer went down. I said, 'Son of a gun! There's a short somewhere that disrupts the power.' There was no power backup on those computers. It was that simple, but we never would have figured it out if we weren't committed to doing everything possible to please our client."

What makes this such an interesting story is that at some point during that weekend trip to the client's office, Michael stopped making money. In fact, it was costing him to be there with all the man-hours he was paying for. **Too many weekends like this and the only system he'd be de-bugging would be his bed at the YMCA.** He could have packed it in at any moment and most people would not have blamed him. When I asked him what he was thinking as he toiled away that whole time, his response was simple and revealing.

"I was thinking, 'I'm creating the best customer I'd ever want.'"

And he was right.

This client was a small business owner, himself. Over the ensuing years he talked about Michael Grottola to many, many people. Some of them eventually became clients themselves. It was, perhaps, his most fruitful relationship as a small business owner—a relationship that ended years later on the best of all possible notes, when the man invited Michael to his retirement party. **His friend's life was now a permanent weekend.**

It was not retirement Michael was thinking about, however, when he decided to get out of the hustle and bustle of self-employment and take a job with more security, greater benefits, and better hours. He and his wife had just adopted two daughters from Russia and he wanted to be there for them as they grew up. So after testing the market, he took a job with consulting giant, KPMG. It would be a pay cut from those fatter small business years during the Reagan and Clinton eras, but his salary would still be well into the six figures and, like I said, it would be secure. It's a decision I understand very well, in fact, as it is the exact reason established actors stop chasing the big movie roles with the huge paydays and start doing television and theater with the smaller, more consistent paychecks. **Give me five seasons of "Boston Legal" and you can keep *Star Trek 14: The Re-Trekkening.***

Despite his expertise in technology and his uniquely valuable skills and experience (to the company), it wasn't long into Michael's stint at KPMG that he got a call from a woman in the Human Resources department. She wanted him to swing by her office for a chat. I've been an actor my entire life, so I've never worked within a rigid corporate structure, but I've starred in enough workplace dramas to know that no one in Human Resources ever just wants to "chat." **They're like doctors. It's fine when you call them, but when *they* call *you*? Look out.**

Michael swung by her office near the end of the day, mentally prepared for whatever might happen. It was a Friday, the end of the workweek, when most companies do their firing. The woman told him to close the door and asked him to sit down. As he settled into the guest chair across from her—a desk covered with manila personnel folders sitting between them—she asked him how he liked his job. He assured her that he liked it very much. The work was interesting, the people were nice, and the pay wasn't too shabby. She nodded along, fully anticipating each of his responses, I'm sure. Then she opened another file folder. His file folder. She scanned it.

"From what I've been told," she began, "you've been a valuable addition to the team since you got here. You've done good work for your department, you've been a team player."

Uh oh, here it comes. The big but....

"But there is an opportunity," she continued, "outside your department, in the company's leadership and management training program. We think you'd be perfect for it. Is that something you might be interested in?"

This wasn't an execution — it was a coronation! Michael exhaled. He could breathe finally. The blood that had drained from his face and pooled in his feet could start circulating again.

"Management?" He asked. "But I'm a technology guy."

"People you work with seem to like you, and you get your work done. That's really all management is." She had a point. Even I could see that, and I can't see anything without my glasses. "Give it some thought and get back to me."

Oh, and mop up that puddle of cold sweat under your chair. Thanks!

So Michael thought about it, talked it over with his wife, and ultimately decided to take them up on their offer. Naturally, he breezed through the training program and then spent the next 13 years in management, gradually taking on more responsibility and earning more money.

The structures of capitalism and the apparatus of Corporate America had worked just like they were designed. They identified talent, put that talent in a position to succeed, and then incentivized that talent to lead other talented people. Things were good. **What could possibly go wrong?**

In a word: 2008. The sub-prime mortgage market collapsed. The housing bubble burst. Major financial institutions teetered on the brink of collapse, triggering massive taxpayer bailouts. As a Canadian,

I am unfamiliar with this kind of malfeasance, but I believe the technical term for it is "total shit-show."

Of course, I don't need to tell you what happened next. You have your 401k statements and home appraisals and blood pressure read-outs from that time to remind you. **(Unless you burned them, like I did.)**

For Michael, it was no different. His home lost a chunk of its value while his mortgage stayed the same. He took a big hit on his savings and retirement money, while the price of college tuition increased with cost of living like it always does. The whole situation cast a great deal of uncertainty over his future.

Unlike many others though, Michael held onto his job. KPMG is a very big company with a lot of institutional clients who need their services and spend a lot of money to procure them. They could sustain a hit like this, for a while.

Unfortunately, the financial crisis continued to drag on and it finally caught up with Michael early in 2009. His boss called him into his office, **and this time it was the bad kind of call.** His boss informed him that he and an entire layer of upper-middle management were being "right-sized." If that isn't the most insulting term ever, I don't know what is. **The only thing that could have made it worse is if it was also Michael's birthday.**

Oh, I forgot to mention, it was also Michael's Birthday.

Being let go sent Michael into a tailspin of depression and self-doubt. What was he going to do? He was 65 years old. He made nearly

$300,000 a year. Nobody was hiring people his age who made that kind of money, if they were even hiring at all. But he needed to work. Not just to pay his mortgage and put his daughters through college, but for his sanity and self-worth.

Michael was 65. He wasn't dead. **A little constipated, maybe, but who isn't?** He had no intention of retiring. He liked his work. He was vital, curious, and active. He was alive. Being "right-sized" made him feel the opposite. They were telling him he was done, that he was wrong-sized. That it was over.

As Michael told me his story, I couldn't help but to flash back to the days after Star Trek ended, because I found myself in a very similar situation. NBC canceled the series after three seasons and immediately I was out of a job. I'd been out of work before, for a week or two here and there, but never for very long. Soon enough a week or two turned into several weeks, which turned into a couple of months. **If you think working's a drag, just try the alternative!**

That's when I realized: what had happened to other actors had finally happened to me.

Like Michael, I had my children's college education to consider, rent to pay and food to put on the table. And that was just the essentials. I had no idea how I was going to make it all work. In the TV world, it's commonly understood that after actors are in a long-running series, they don't work for a while. It can be months, sometimes a year. If you played a well-known character in a TV series, like Captain Kirk, you may not appear on another series for *years*.

It's like the studios were following their own version of the Prime Directive: they wouldn't interfere with my lack of an income.

Although I didn't realize it way back when, I took a page from this book I'm writing here to pull myself out of the hole into which Star Trek's cancellation had hurled me. I marshaled my intuition, my instincts for self-preservation, and the collective wisdom born of years of experience and took my family's needs into my own hands.

In those days, they wrote plays with one set and 3 or 4 or 5 actors. They would play Broadway for a year or two and the plays would go out and make Samuel French's playwright list and Samuel would rent them out, paying a few dollars to each of the playwrights. It was cheap enough to produce and if a play was good enough to warrant putting it on in summer stock, some good actors would do it. They'd go out and play all the small theaters. People in their summer homes, on vacation, or just driving out on a Sunday, would come to the theater in rather respectable numbers. Imagine that: **America, a country of theatergoers!**

I'd written plays before. I'd worked on the stage as well as the small screen. I knew comedy and drama. I was great at memorizing lines so I always knew everybody's parts. Hell, I was kind of a one-man production company. So that's what I did. I used everything in my tool kit and put together little plays with myself as the lead, somebody else as well-known as possible playing the other part and we would pick up actors where we could. We'd go 13, 15, 17 weeks, every week in a different theater. We'd move in, play all week and on Saturday night, strike the set, and get into our cars and head out to the next theater down the road – maybe 100 or 300 miles away.

I did that for three summers. Me, my Doberman pinscher named Morgan, and a pick-up truck with oversized tires that I prayed would hold out. By forgoing motels during those thirteen summer weeks and instead sleeping in the back of my truck under the camper shell I had mounted, I was able to save enough money by Labor Day each year to fund my children's education, rent, food and clothes. The little bit left over for me was barely enough to pay for popcorn. But boy did that popcorn taste good. **I think Morgan liked it, too.**

There are two things you can do when you hit rock bottom. You can splat against it or you can bounce back off it. I bounced back. And I realize now, telling this story, that I did it by essentially hiring myself. With the specter of extended unemployment hanging over me, I put my skills and experience to work for three years, doing summer stock across the country. And not only did I provide for my family, but I emerged a stronger person for it. Then, before you know it, I was back working on television and the movies. **From a pickup truck to a network pickup letter. Only in America!**

Michael Grottola took a similar route. He chose to bounce back off the bottom. He collected himself and started to take stock of everything he had going for him.

He had a degree in engineering and expertise in software, **neither of which had gone out of style.**

He had 13 fruitful years in management, so he knew how to lead people and manage projects.

He'd started his own lucrative business once upon a time, so he understood risk and entrepreneurship. More importantly, he was comfortable with them.

He'd saved a good amount of money and built a solid credit history over the years, **so he could be his own ATM for a while.**

It turns out Michael had a lot going for him. These were assets, literally and figuratively, that no one could take away from him like KPMG had taken his job. They were his, the product of decades of work and experience. Now the only question was, what to do with them?

As I got older, I wrestled with this same question. When jobs ended I struggled with what to do with all the assets and experience I'd accrued over the years. I could put myself back into the meat grinder of the traditional Hollywood system like any other actor looking for work, but the auditions and offers for an actor in his 60s are fewer and farther between, so I would have been subjecting myself not just to the law of diminishing returns but also to the humiliation of constant rejection. In the military, they call that a "soup sandwich."

Michael was in a similar position in 2009/2010. The job market for well-paid workers closing in on retirement age looked like the soupiest of soup sandwiches. And kudos to Michael, he had no interest in taking a bite. He wasn't going to play their game only to be entertained, patronized and shown the door; both parties to the interview knowing full well that he didn't have a snowball's chance in Phoenix of booking the gig (in the parlance of show business).

Taking stock of his assets, Michael realized he had a lot of very useful knowledge and experience that people could profit from. His years as a successful entrepreneur combined with his years inside one of the world's foremost consulting firms made him the perfect candidate to start his own consulting business. **In other words, by firing Michael, KPMG didn't just lose an asset. They created a competitor.**

Now, if you're like me, you probably don't have a solid grasp on what exactly consulting is. I know I didn't. So I asked Andy Stefanovich, a business consultant for numerous Fortune 100 companies from Richmond, Virginia who started a wonderful little consulting business called "Play!" back in the '90s that he sold to a bigger consulting firm called Prophet a few years ago.

"A consultant," he told me, "is someone who is an expert in a particular field or area of business that companies hire when they don't have that expertise in house."

"So Bob Routt, who was one of our technical advisers on T.J. Hooker, he was a consultant?"

"Exactly," Andy explained. "He was an expert in police procedures that you guys hired because you were TV people doing a cop show, not cops doing a TV show. If this were the business world, he would have his own consulting firm, or consultancy, which is basically just the business you build around your expertise."

Pretty sweet when you can be both the owner of a business and its main product. You know you'll never run out of stock!

Initially, Michael Grottola thought about focusing his consultancy around technology. He was an engineer after all, and he was great with software. But that idea didn't light a fire inside him. Besides, there were thousands of that type of consultant all over the world and most of them operated on the very front edge of technology, where he decidedly was not after a decade plus in management. What really got Michael going was the idea of helping aspiring entrepreneurs, young and old, realize their dream of starting their own small business.

With decades under his belt as a successful small business owner, then in management in Corporate America, Michael was ideally suited to help entrepreneurs avoid getting chewed up and spit out by their respective industries. He understood the importance of hard work because it was the difference between getting paid and getting fired when he first went out on his own. He recognized good ideas when he saw them because it was the companies built around good ideas that could ultimately afford the services of his previous employer, KPMG. He knew what investors were looking for and he had a feel for where the market was headed; why do you think he got into technology way back in the late '60s and early '70s? With his skillset and wisdom—his expertise—he could help these fledgling companies learn from his experiences so they didn't have to live them themselves. **He could be like a veteran athlete taking a rookie under his wing, minus the part about changing in front of each other.**

So, in the early fall of 2009, Michael Grottola opened a consultancy dedicated to helping aspiring entrepreneurs find funding for their business ideas. He would help them put together their business plans, their investment proposals and loan applications. He would help them refine their pitches and coach them on how to best express their value proposition. This was new territory for Michael—telling people what they should do and getting paid for it—but one he was comfortable finding his way through.

Perhaps unsurprisingly, in the beginning the bulk of Michael's expertise came through the wisdom he gained from thirty years of hard work. **It turns out you learn a lot when you're too busy to notice!**

"I tell them," Michael said, "to be an entrepreneur, you have to take risks. You have to say, 'I will expect an income that is few and far between in the beginning. I have to live with spotty cash flow. I have to persuade people, demonstrate value. I have to deal with a myriad of things that someone who has a job and is employed doesn't ever think of.' You also have to work around the clock; weekends, nights. Work your butt off. There's a reason it's called 'sweat equity.' If you're a forty hour a week person, don't even start."

Tough love, delivered with a smile - and an invoice.

His advice did not fall on deaf ears. By the end of the year—with less than six months in business—he'd made his first $30,000. It was a fraction of what he would have made at KPMG in that same period. When I asked Michael if that worried him, if it made him regret his choice to go out on his own, this was his answer:

"I was happy as a clam."

He had bounced back. He was alive.

Do you recognize aspects of yourself in Michael Grotolla's story? It doesn't matter if it's his age, the circumstances of his firing from KPMG (I refuse to dignify it with a term like "right-sized"), his early work history, his heritage or geography, even his choice of fields. What matters, if you relate even a little to Michael's story, is to ask yourself the same questions and take the same inventory he did when he felt like he'd hit the bottom.

What do you have going for you?

What are you good at?

What can you teach the next generation that they need to know?

Who is counting on you?

What drives you with a fire so hot it burns the inside of your t-shirt?

Most of you out there over 50 years old who are trying to bounce back, or find your next thing for the next phase of your life, have answers to these questions that make a consultancy a real, viable option for you. It is not: if being a consultant makes sense, it's what kind of consultant will be the most rewarding personally and financially. Piecing together your answers to these questions around whatever goals you have for the next phase of your life will go a long way to figuring that out.

Of course the road ahead is not paved with sunshine and kittens. **Unlike movie tickets,** there is no AARP discount rate for success. You have to earn it. And like Michael tells his start-up clients, you'll have to work your butt off. If you don't want to do that—which no one will begrudge you in the least—then maybe a consulting business is not for you. If you're up for the challenge though, the payoff is clear.

In late 2009, at his lowest point, Michael Grottola said "Enough!" He took everything he had learned, all his wisdom and expertise from decades of experience, and chose to put it to work for himself.

By 2013, Michael had multiple full-time employees, more than 40 regular paying clients, and annual net profit at or above his salary at the time he was let go. **As far as Michael was concerned, KPMG now stood for "Keep Plugging, Michael Grotolla!"**

I'll never forget my reaction when Michael told me how happy he was in those first few months on his own. Happy as a clam? Really!? I was shocked. Almost as shocked as he was confused by my question.

"But weren't you scared?" I asked.

He chuckled. "Of course I was scared. But I was more scared of doing something I didn't like. Or worse, doing nothing and withering away."

I talked to dozens of people over 50 for this book and almost to the man (and woman) they acknowledged the fear and in the same breath talked about how happy they were to have faced it down.

They would never go back to Corporate America, to the 9-to-5 rat race. Not a single one of them. They couldn't imagine their lives any other way.

In chapter after chapter, you'll hear from inventors, writers, franchisees, small business owners, web-masters, and coaches. All of them will say some version of the same thing. And you will see in them aspects of yourselves that I hope spark you to take the leap, to bounce back, to live. By hiring yourself.

CHAPTER TWO

FROM BURNOUT TO BUSINESS OWNER: RECOGNIZING OPPORTUNITY AND SEIZING IT

Full Shatner Interview: CatchMeUp.com/Thomas & CatchMeUp.com/Dave

In all his years managing the West Marine store in Portland, Oregon, Thomas Betts had never had a request quite like this. Amid the monotony of GPS units and lifejackets, a man walked in off the street asking for 500 feet of thick rope.

"Five hundred feet?" Betts asked. "That's a lot of boats."

"I don't own boats," the man replied, leaving Betts temporarily befuddled.

Thomas was hesitant to ask why on earth someone could need that much rope. For one thing, if Clue and Law & Order: SVU have taught us anything it's that a rope can be used for any number of less than friendly or G-rated purposes. But more importantly, as an experienced salesman, he knew once you've made the sale you stop talking and head to the cash register. **Pervert or not, the man's a customer.** And this fellow was sold before he walked in the store. Betts kept up his friendly banter as they completed the transaction, but eventually his curiosity got the better of him. *If it wasn't for mooring the entire 5th Fleet, he thought, then what?*

"I have to ask, what are you going to do with all that rope?"

"Alpacas," said the buyer. It was the second time in five minutes Betts didn't know what to say. "It's for tying up alpacas," the man clarified. The ship rope was the only kind that was sturdy enough to tie up the animals but also thick enough that it wouldn't cut off their circulation and potentially harm them. It was the strangest request Thomas had filled in a long time and even though he got his answer from the customer, all it did was create more questions.

Questions like, *How many alpacas do you have? Where did you get them? And, most of all, What the hell is an alpaca?*

Betts was not a rancher; he was a sea dog. He loved being on the water. In his spare time, he raced a 41-foot sailboat. The sleek, gorgeous vessel was the site of numerous family sailing trips and celebrations over the years. Being general manager of a boating equipment store allowed him to combine his work with his passion—with a discount no less. A veteran of the business, Thomas took his job seriously. He prided himself on both his honesty and his sales savvy. Being a salesman, said Betts, "is about helping people meet their needs. Listening to them, what their needs are, and trying to fulfill those needs. My goal was to make sure they were happy by the time they walked out of the store." **Naturally, management hated him. But more on that in a minute.**

The guy with the alpacas, and now the 500 feet of rope, he'd had his needs met, he was happy. Thomas Betts, however, couldn't say the same. He loved boats, sure, but it couldn't make up for what he *didn't* love: the corporate environment that came with managing his West Marine branch. He understood that every store in a franchise needs to make money—the real world isn't like Hollywood—but over time he'd grown disillusioned with the laser focus on "making the numbers," as his superiors put it. Every day was like that Dunkin' Donuts commercial from the mid-1980s: *time to make the donuts, I made the donuts, time to make the donuts, I made the donuts.* **(And if you don't remember that ad, you might be too young for this book!)** All Thomas' bosses wanted was to make sure that more and more products were sold, that there was always "more growth" and "bigger targets". What frustrated Betts so much was that none of these metrics were tied to any of the more important things in life: happiness, family, relationships, and general contentment.

The sailor's spirits were sinking.

"Our biggest day of the year was always the 4th of July," Betts told me the first time we sat down to chat at a radio station in Los Angeles. "If it fell on a weekend, we'd do very well. Everybody would be happy. But next year, 4th of July might be on a weekday, and if there wasn't a special sale to make up for it, our total sales wouldn't be as good. And then Corporate would want to know why we didn't do as well." **That was like asking why the snow cones didn't sell on a rainy day, but management didn't care.** They wanted to point fingers instead; a reality made even more frustrating by the fact that Thomas had no control over solving a problem that directly affected his compensation.

A large part of Betts' pay was tied to a bonus based on sales revenues. For Thomas, this was a bit of a Catch-22, because Corporate determined the marketing strategies the store would use to help drive sales. He could ignore his bosses and do it his way, potentially increasing the sales that would increase his bonus. But flouting their rules and implicitly denigrating their strategies could also lead to trouble — **discipline, loss of his bonus, or even firing. Like a crewman on a poorly captained vessel,** there was nothing he could do to **change course.** Corporate wasn't interested in his suggestions on how to make their sales strategies more effective, or what kind of marketing needed to be done to make sure customers came to the store. The whole song-and-dance began to wear on Betts. He loved boats, he loved being on the water and he loved the marine industry, but he'd had enough of this annual ebb and flow over which he had almost zero control.

Betts toyed with getting out a number of times that year, but a few things always stood in his way. He was over 50, for one, which in this day and age automatically makes it harder to find a well-paying job. He had a family to support, too, with a mortgage and an expensive hobby to boot. Competitive sailing is no joke, I've come to learn. **The boats may be powered by wind, but they're made out of money.** Thomas' job at West Marine provided the steady employment that allowed him to pay the bills, support his family and keep a foothold in the world of sailing, his main passion. Finding another job that could do all that and make him happier? Well that was an even taller order.

Still, the urge to escape the rat race gnawed at him during the entire drive home that day. He couldn't stop thinking about the man with the alpacas. He knew his wife, Connie, grew up around farm animals, maybe she would know what the heck they were. When he came through the door that evening, Connie, who worked at home as a technical writer, began the idle chit-chat that is familiar to so many of us married couples.

"How was your day?" she asked. "How was work?"

"I had some guy come in and ask for 500 feet of rope for tying up alpacas," he said. "Ever heard of them?"

Connie's eyes lit up in a way that Thomas had never seen before. An avid knitter, Connie liked the sturdy yarn alpaca fibers produced. And she thought the animals themselves were cute, in their own goofy way.

"What does he do?" she asked. "Does he breed them?"

Thomas shrugged.

"Where does he have them?" she asked.

"He's over in Hood River."

Connie's eyes lit up again. Hood River is on the other side of the Cascade Mountain range – the sunny side. **Portland was a great city, but sometimes it seemed like there was a civic ordinance forbidding suntans. Just an hour east, though, they enjoy 50 percent more sunlight each year.** The Betts had always thought about living over there but never made the jump what with Thomas' job and his sailboat and their abiding love of the water. Still, the bug never left them. The sunny side of the Cascades always called to them. This alpaca thing was starting to feel like something that could fulfill a couple of dreams.

"Does he make a living off of them?" Connie continued.

"He says he does. Hey, what is an alpaca anyway?"

The couple took to the Internet and spent the rest of the evening researching the animals. A cousin to the llama, alpacas are an intelligent, highly trainable camel-type species that are, better still, very low maintenance. At this point in their lives Thomas and Connie had no interest in waking up at 2am to head out onto the farm like many of the fruit growers and ranchers over in the Hood River Valley, so a more demanding animal would have made the idea a non-starter. Instead, the more they learned about alpaca ranching and the businesses that have sprung up around the industry, the **more these sailors started to consider the landlubber lifestyle.** But how many people actually do this and make a living?

It turned out that the alpaca community in the United States was vast. There was a wide network of breeders, farms and other associated businesses across the country, selling the livestock and the fibers that could be woven from the animals' fur. The pioneering farmers who imported the first alpacas into the United States in 1984 were even running seminars on how to turn raising alpacas into a business. **Who knew? Maybe alpaca farming is what all those theatergoers from the 1960s got into.** It began to feel like maybe the stars were aligning for them.

Their interest now more than piqued, the couple attended one of these seminars in nearby Portland. While it was surely not as exciting as a Star Trek convention, the Betts liked what they saw, so much so that they began to seriously weigh the decision to raise alpacas full-time.

"The return on investment seemed worth it," said Thomas. "But still, there was that looming thought – we could go bust." **But hey, even if they lost everything, at least they could knit themselves some loin cloths.**

Rather than making a drastic change, the Betts waded into the world of alpacas in measured steps. Thomas was still holding down his old job. West Marine was his safety net, in case this roll of the dice proved unfavorable, and you don't pull that net away until you've crossed the gap or you can at least see the other side. Their first step out onto the high wire was the sale of their home and the purchase of a property in Hood River, where the terrain was ideal for alpacas to graze. If you're like me when you first read that sentence, you're probably wondering who in their right mind thinks that, of all things, is a measured first step? They'd had their suburban Portland home for years. Their children grew up in it. They had Christmases there. It was full of history and memories. But when Thomas explained their decision it made perfect sense: the property they found was a great price, it was big enough for everything they would need—a barn, a home, pasture--and it would fulfill Connie's desire to move out to the country. So if the alpaca business did go bust, they wouldn't have broken the bank buying the property and they'd be living somewhere they'd always wanted to be. Plus, he'd still have his job at West Marine, even if the commute was now a little longer.

"From work to Hood River was about an hour and fifteen minutes," Thomas said in what I came to understand was his typical glass half-full approach to this new life. "Nearly twice as long from our old place. But you know, you've got to drive along the river, it's a beautiful drive, and you're not fighting the traffic. That's a pleasant thing to have." **As a part-time resident of the 101 freeway, I found this outlook refreshing, to say the least.**

Around this time, Thomas also started working on his former customer's alpaca farm; you remember, the man who needed 500 feet of rope. He offered Thomas a part-time job and Thomas, who was keen to learn the business from the ground up, readily accepted. What better way to learn than with someone who'd already done it? His early days were spent doing menial tasks. **Alpacas are cute, but wool isn't the only thing they produce. So Thomas began by** cleaning the barn and shoveling manure; "touching the ground" jobs, so to speak. He observed the animals and watched how the actual business was run – he was truly working his way up the ladder so that when he and Connie had a farm of their own, he would know how to solve any possible issue that could arise.

As I reflected back on Thomas's description of those early stages in their move toward alpaca farming, I was struck by how often I heard similar stories from the other over-50 entrepreneurs you will meet in this book. Almost to the person, no matter the business, they planned and tested and analyzed and then they worked their butts off. There was never any ego, they got down in the dirt with their own two hands—in Thomas's case, quite literally so—and carved out a space for themselves until they had something that was working, something they could call their own.

So be like Thomas. Find your own alpaca farm – whatever it may be – and shovel the crap out of it!

For Thomas and Connie though, getting their hands dirty wasn't going to be enough. They had to figure out a way to finance this venture. For Connie's part, she kept her job as a technical writer, because it allowed them to maintain a reliable income and **she could do it from their fledgling farmland there in the Hood River Valley.** But Thomas had bigger plans. He was going to sell his beloved 41-foot sailboat—something to which the family was dearly attached.

"My kids thought we were nuts," said Thomas, "to give this all up for a hairy animal with long eyelashes." I knew exactly how

Thomas felt. I got a very similar reaction from my children when we bought our place in Kentucky and started raising horses. All I'd ever done was act, that's all they knew. Who was this man who looked like their father but had all these horses around?!? I understood their reservations. But once my children recognized that I had found something that truly energized me, they were fully supportive. Thomas and Connie were, no doubt, in a similar situation. **Economists talk about "animal spirits" that drive people to take risks. Well, sometimes, there are actual animals involved!**

With their kids support, the Betts took the proceeds from Thomas's sailboat and bought seven alpacas—four females and three males. Overnight their new property on the sunny side of the Cascades went from farmland to just farm. Little by little, the farm grew. They began to breed, show, and sell the alpacas. Then Royal Dutch, their first stud, won a major show in Louisville and slingshot the Betts farm into the media spotlight. Royal Dutch quickly became in high demand among other alpaca farmers for his breeding potential. With every healthy offspring he produced and every prize he won at an alpaca show, his reputation as a stud grew – and that meant more money for the Betts. Nine months later, with his frustration with the corporate world at its highest, Thomas decided his alpaca business was doing well enough that he could "make the cross-over." He undid the safety net and quit his "day job" at West Marine.

Royal Dutch wasn't the only one feeling like a stud that day.

Breeding alpacas was proving to be a successful venture, but there wasn't enough money in it to make that alone a full-time job. The Betts decided to diversify their business and take advantage of multiple revenue streams by selling the fibers that come from the alpaca's coat. They developed working relationships with local businesses like Pendleton Mills, an Oregon-based purveyor of high-end clothing. According to Thomas, their alpaca products are hot sellers, with everything from socks to blankets to sweaters being produced from the naturally insulating alpaca fiber. At Connie's suggestion, the couple also opened a small store on their farm where not only do they sell their own alpaca yarn, but they sell the knitwear produced by Pendleton Mills with the alpaca fiber purchased wholesale from their very own farm. They make money on the fiber coming and going. It's an ingenious set-up and one only someone with extensive experience in sales who was also prepared to seize every available opportunity coming his way could have recognized.

The Betts have utilized community engagement as another way to market their farm. Visitors to the Hood River Valley can take a tour of the farm as part of the Hood River Fruit Loop, an organization of farms, vineyards, and artisan shops. This tour can bring in as many as two bus-loads full of visitors at a time to experience the animals for themselves, learn about the workings of the farm, and visit the on-site store. Thomas is also able to help other would-be alpaca ranchers get off the ground by sharing his expertise. "That's where I get really excited," he says, "helping other people become successful.

And it's only fair. After all, a few years ago Thomas didn't know an alpaca from Al Pacino!

And how are the Betts doing as a result of their seemingly risky, life-changing venture? According to the couple, they've never been better off financially. And they're happier than ever too.

"I didn't know what an alpaca was until I had that customer come into my store," says Thomas. "Now, I've fallen in love. I am around the animals every day, and people too. They love the alpacas, and I get to see that. I get to help people who come to me, asking how they can make this kind of change in their life."

Animal spirits, indeed.

But Thomas also cautions that alpacas are a rather unique proposition. "They don't eat a lot, they are smart animals – they poop in a dedicated spot – their vet bills aren't very big, but you have to look at all the expenses and see if it works. In our case, it did, but it's not always that easy."

In talking about this subject during my travels in various capacities around the country, Thomas' story resonated with a lot of people—especially men tired or bored of just comfortably getting by doing the same drudgery every day. They asked me how he did it and honestly, in the moment, I wasn't exactly sure.

I think he asked himself the right questions:

Are you happy?

Where do you want to be?

What kind of risks are you really willing to take?

How important is money?

What kind of assets do you have that you can leverage?

Then I think he answered them honestly and acted accordingly. If the Betts' change was motivated by both financial gain and a chance to live a better lifestyle, then our next subject changed his life in the name of his own survival.

Dave Bateman had plenty of money, but was completely burned out. With nearly four decades of legal experience under his belt, Bateman had slowly watched his faith in the legal profession **wither** in front of his eyes. He became increasingly disillusioned and, as the moral and ethical **level of his profession** fell, his stress levels rose. The job he used to love was now taking a toll on his physical and spiritual health.

I know what you're thinking: When was the legal profession ever moral and ethical? Maybe it never was, but the effect on Dave was cumulative.

"Forget the law, forget the purity of the law. It's about getting the results," he told me, almost as soon as we sat down. "Many attorneys today you'll find are business, business, business: We will do, we will say, we will conjure up whatever story we need for the client. Don't worry so much about the truth. That's not important. You use the system to get the results."

As a deeply religious man with an unflappable moral compass, Bateman began to question whether the current climate was one in which he even felt comfortable practicing.

"Even at 67, I'm still an idealist," he said. "I just believe the law is amazing. The law can solve problems, but if you abuse the law, just like if you abuse medicine or drugs, it's not going to work. The system will fail."

Abusing the law is like abusing alcohol and drugs? That makes sense — I've had lawyers who abused all three!

In the end, the decision was made for him. Bateman ended up in the hospital with heart palpitations, a condition likely brought on by his own stress. It was his first serious health crisis, and for Dave and his wife Trudy, it was a much needed wakeup call. Dave wasn't the only one who felt as if he was running on the ragged edge. Trudy was an ER nurse, and after 38 years on the job, she had seen enough trauma and tragedy to last a lifetime. The couple started to seriously consider retirement.

Then, just like in the movies, a trip to Hawaii changed everything.

One of Dave's clients called him up to discuss some real estate contracts on the Big Island. This was nothing new, given that the man owned properties all over the world. "Dave, get on an airplane and come over," he said, "I just bought a couple coffee farms."

Going to Hawaii "on business" is one of life's great accidental luxuries, and the couple didn't even think twice about making the trip. A little time in the sun and salt air was just what they needed. When the Batemans arrived in Kona, they were awestruck. Dave's eyes grew wide as he took in the newly purchased farm's 360-degree view of the ocean and the nearby village. His client seemed to be gauging Dave's reaction as they walked through the coffee trees. Finally he asked, "What do you think?"

"This is pretty cool," Dave responded. Everything about this farm looked good; definitely a sound investment.

"Dave, you're going to buy this."

Bateman looked up at his client, expecting to see him chuckle over the joke. Instead he saw the man's finger pointed right at him. "Okay boss," he said. "Hey Trudy, we're going to buy a coffee farm." Dave's wife rolled her eyes.

But his client was serious. Even he could see that Dave needed a change and he was willing to turn the contracts over to the Batemans, giving the couple a chance to start over in an idyllic location. Slowly, this realization dawned on Dave.

His own *client* wanted him to get out of the legal swamp, and was willing to scuttle his own deal to make it happen? What planet was this? Hawaii, apparently.

The idea of running a 38-acre coffee farm was intimidating to a man whose coffee IQ extended only as far as his usual Starbucks order. Still, Dave's emotional response to the farm was one he couldn't ignore. So after decades of following only reason, logic, and the letter of the law, he made a decision based on what he felt. "I fell in love. I just knew in my heart that it was the right thing to do." And that was it. The Batemans bought two coffee farms and moved to **paradise.**

In many ways, the Batemans had a storybook ending to their

old life, and began their new one with a huge leg up. There were minimal start-up costs, and the particular coffee grown on Kona was also in very high demand. Better still, the particular farm they were moving to was considered one of the best coffee producers in the region, having won more awards than this book can recount. "I felt it was a fairly safe deal," said Dave, "because the previous owner had won many awards. I knew the potential was there." But for two urban professionals without a lick of experience it wasn't exactly a winning lottery ticket.

Bateman truly felt that he could bring the farm's coffee to the next level; the question was "How?" He still knew nothing about farming. **The closest Dave had ever come to agricultural work was mowing his lawn, and he hadn't even done that lately.** As he stood in his new house, looking over the 38 acres that now belonged to him, Dave couldn't help but wonder: "How am I supposed to do this?"

Before he set out for his first day in the fields, Dave read up extensively on coffee farming and techniques, soaking up as much knowledge as he could. He applied the same zeal and work ethic to his new vocation as he had in his earlier years with the law. Even so, it wasn't a substitute for practical experience. Luckily for him, the old owner of the farm agreed to act as Dave's mentor. The Air Force veteran and (until just recently) high-powered attorney was about to get an education in how to drive a tractor, fertilize the land, and fix irrigation lines. But first he'd have to learn the ropes, working in the fields to pick, prune and sucker the coffee beans alongside the other laborers.

As Dave was learning, growing coffee is hard work. That's why they can charge $5 a cup for the stuff.

Outside the farm, however, Dave was able to let the talents from his past life flourish. Bateman quickly got himself elected to local coffee boards and began networking with farmers and other coffee industry types in the area. Dave and Trudy didn't know a soul in their new tropical retirement paradise, and it was comforting to have a network of friends who knew how to guide them through all the challenges farming would throw at them.

On the mainland, it's easy to call up a friend or colleague when faced with a work problem. But Hawaii's isolation adds another layer of complexity, one that Dave was initially unprepared for. It took a major mechanical breakdown on the farm for Dave to realize just how self-reliant he'd need to be if he was going to make it.

"Last year our wet mill sheered a shaft, which means we were out of business. I didn't have a replacement for it, so one of my employees and I had to take it apart and figure it out for ourselves. Especially in Hawaii, you can't just call and say, "Ship me a part tomorrow." It's a week to two weeks to get parts." Dave ended up having to build a new one with the help of his neighbor. He simply could not afford to wait for a new part to be shipped in, and had to rely on himself as well as his new friends to help him through the crisis. **He'd gone from shafting people to building his own drive shaft — pretty neat!**

Despite these setbacks, Dave was driven to succeed in his new industry. He powered through the learning curve. And for all of their hard work, the Bateman's farm is now thriving. "We've won an award every year, " Dave tells me, "and this year we are the reigning champion for Kona and the entire state of Hawaii. We beat out 170 other farms."

Despite coming from vastly different walks of life, both Thomas Betts and Dave Bateman found themselves in fairly similar situations. Despite being in the prime of their respective lives, the two men were unsatisfied with their current situation and felt that a change was necessary. Both had secure, fairly stable jobs that paid the bills, and changing careers was a risky venture. **People thought they were crazy.**

Rather than jumping in with both feet, the two took a measured, deliberate approach to their transition. Each man entered into a business that already had a strong customer base built into it. Neither required significant resources to bring their plan to fruition, nor did their respective businesses require a substantial effort to market and sell their products. As different as they may be, the market for Kona coffee and alpaca fibers exists both at home and abroad, with customers ready to snap up the products. **In fact, there's probably someone sipping a cup of the Bateman's coffee while knitting from a ball of Betts' alpaca yarn right now.**

But rather than simply rest on selling their core products, both Betts and Bateman decided to diversify their business and build multiple revenue streams. The Betts' alpaca farm offers the couple a number of ways to do this, from breeding opportunities (selling the offspring and putting their males out to stud), sales of the alpaca fibers (both at their on-site store and to apparel companies) and by offering farm tours and a petting zoo for visitors who are touring the area.

Diversifying in this manner is a good way to insulate your business from economic shocks – something that the Batemans are more exposed to, as they operate on a much more narrow focus. They offer tours and coffee tastings to supplement their business. Having these alternatives on hand is crucial for their coffee farm, since there are so many natural threats that can harm their plantation. **For instance, meet the beetles.**

"Coffee farms", says Dave Bateman, "are vulnerable to a lot of invasive species. This year, and the last three years, we've been suffering from coffee berry bore damage, which is a beetle that came in from Panama. I don't know how it got here, but it drills into the coffee bean, into the cherry and into the coffee bean itself and lays larvae. Our farm has suffered about a 20 percent loss. We have 900 farms in Kona, with 4000 acres planted, and half of our farms suffered over the last two years. We have estimated as much as 50 to 100 percent losses because of this bug."

If something were taking away 50 to 100 percent of *my* coffee — to say nothing of my livelihood — I'd be a lot more panicked than Dave seems to be.

With the life experience that you've accumulated over the last five, six or seven decades on this planet, you understand as well as anyone else how important it is to be able to cope with setbacks – and that you can't always do it alone.

Both Dave Betts and Thomas Bateman are extraordinarily lucky to have supportive spouses who have been there for them every step of the way. Both Connie Betts and Trudy Bateman knew that their husbands were unhappy in their current situation. **Maybe — and I'm just speculating here — these men's unhappiness had made them a *tad* hard to live with.** Whatever the case, when it came time to make that change, both of them not only stood by their husbands' decision, but encouraged them to try something new. They even took proactive roles in getting the new businesses off the ground.

For Thomas, it was Connie's experience growing up around farm animals that proved integral to helping the couple become successful alpaca ranchers. While Thomas had to learn the ropes on his own, Connie was able to tend to their new property while working from home. That allowed Connie to bring both income and practical experience to the table, and make the transition to their new life as smooth as possible.

And as burnt out as Dave Bateman was, his wife Trudy was feeling the pressure as well. Whatever ethical or moral deficiencies there were in the legal world, Trudy's job in the ER was a daily litany of unpleasant situations ranging from gruesome to tragic. Dave's health problems forced Trudy to examine her own quality of life. She realized that something had to give.

These women weren't spectators. They were copilots.

Speaking of copilots, the Bateman's, like many Americans, sought guidance from above when it came time to make the big leap. Both Dave and Trudy are proud Christians, and a decision as big as this needed to be prayed over.

"I put a lot of stock on the Lord. A lot of my life's decisions I consult, I pray every day, and I prayed into this, and I just felt at peace," he said. "You develop that peace, that quiet inner peace in your heart, and you just know the little issues will work themselves out, and that's the sense that I had. I was totally at peace. I can't explain it, other than it was a revelation."

Even though he was unsure of whether it was the right move, or if he even wanted to be a coffee farmer, his deep faith allowed him to see out the move, and step away from the kind of life that wasn't bringing him the inner peace he desired so much.

When a smart, motivated man gets help from his wife and his God — watch out.

"I didn't know the first thing about coffee when I got here. I had not yet developed that feeling of passion for the farm. I just knew I had to make a change. Now, I have a passion. I love what I'm doing. That's critical. You read all the articles about business and if you don't have a passion for it, you're not going to succeed. You're going to have to persevere and persist through the ups and downs."

For the Batemans, their strong spiritual grounding helped them turn a totally alien subject – coffee – into a love that works hand in hand with their devotion and appreciation for the divine. Buoyed by the overriding sense that "the Lord will provide," they shed their former life, where cynicism and dishonesty reigned, and started anew in a faraway location.

Since the move, the Batemans have built on their faith as they have built on their business. They've gotten more involved in Christian causes and local issues on the island—he even ran for the State House of Representatives in 2012. But most importantly for Dave, he is more content, less stressed and closer to God.

It also helps that he hired a first-rate employee — himself.

CHAPTER THREE

SUPERHIGHWAY TO SUPERSTORE: EVOLVING A BUSINESS ONTO THE INTERNET

Full Shatner Interview: CatchMeUpv.com/Julie & CatchMeUp.com/Geri

The mid-1990s was a period of great transition. Not only did they kill off Captain Kirk in Star Trek: Generations but Al Gore also managed to invent the Internet while running for and then serving as Vice President of the United States. Obviously some of that's not true, but what is true was the introduction and explosion of the commercial Internet during this period. So many of the digital things we take for granted in our daily lives today can trace their roots back to these years, that the impact of the Internet can hardly be overstated. **I even heard about an online company that lets people name their own price for airline tickets. How crazy is *that*?**

Still, since we over-50s have lived most of our lives prior to the popularization of the World Wide Web, it's been relatively easy for us to dismiss its importance. I count myself as no exception, at least at first. For instance, I paid no attention when someone bought WilliamShatner.com in 1998. Then a few years later, when I realized this Internet place was going to be a thing, I forked over $1500 to get it for myself. I had to learn the hard way, and learning new things is hard as you get older. Especially when it comes to grappling with the endless march of ever-more invasive, "intuitive" technology: social networks, apps, games, and smartphones. The knee-jerk reaction for many folks our age is to leave those shiny, glowing devices for our kids and grandkids to tinker around with. **If we need something to read on the train or in the bathroom, well, that's what Guttenberg made books for.**

For the longest time, Julie Cole looked upon the Internet on a need-to-know basis: when it came to online technology, the 66 year-old had decided she simply didn't need to know. Based in the small town of Jefferson, Ohio with her husband of 37 years, it wasn't until she started her third business in 2006, Perfect Rubber Mulch, that Julie realized she needed a website to advertise the tire-based ground covering product designed for playgrounds and landscaping.

At the time, Julie was simply the middle-woman. She had a distributor-type relationship with the mulch manufacturer – an old-fashioned guy with no cell phone and no email address – who was happy to give her as much mulch as her heart desired. And she had a wholesale/retail company set up out of her home to take orders from businesses and individuals looking to buy the product for their own use. This was not a high-margin business, and Julie understood that, but working from home as a one-woman operation in a business that didn't yet have a lot of competition put her in great position to make a healthy profit. Everything was in place for Perfect Rubber Mulch to establish a monopoly within a niche market. **It may not have been Boardwalk and Park Place, but she was ready to start building.**

There was one problem: sales volume. Julie knew there were only so many people who would think to look for Perfect Rubber Mulch in the phone book, let alone purchase large quantities of the product over the phone without at least having some way to see it. She didn't have a store, so that eliminated the possibility of telling prospective customers to hop in the car and come check out the goods. Plus, having a store eliminated the virtues of being a middle-woman and probably would have eaten up her entire profit margin. Fairly quickly, she sensed that the old methods of finding businesses were dying out, and that if her business didn't exist online, it simply wouldn't exist in the eyes of the greater population. "People wonder why they fail when they don't put themselves out there, and don't grow with the economics of the world," she told me. "You have to grow." Going online and putting up a website would be the way to do it.

This presented a second problem: **Julie was born in 1948, back when being a "webmaster" meant having eight legs and eating flies.** She knew nothing about the Internet or how to create a website. Starting from scratch, she set about learning everything she could find on the topic: books dedicated to web development, online courses, and web-based seminars conducted by experts in the field. She wasn't afraid to admit that she knew nothing about this topic; instead, Julie became a sponge **soaking** up as many insights as possible, so that she could expand her business opportunities beyond the local phone book to a global audience.

Little by little, her knowledge and confidence grew, developing to the point where she had created a rudimentary website using Microsoft FrontPage and hosted it online. It wasn't the most attractive web destination in the world, but it served its purpose, containing a few photos and several pages that described the product and the business. Most important, though, was the call-to-action: a phone number for potential rubber mulch customers to call at any time. On the other end of the line, they'd find Julie Cole: **proprietor, head saleswoman and unlikely Webmaster – the two-legged kind.**

While we all love to hear about overnight success stories, I'd be lying if I painted Julie's as one of those. Even with the Perfect Rubber Mulch website in place, it took several years for her to build her sales volume to a respectable level. "It took a lot of time," she told me. "You don't just go on the internet and put up a website; it's not a matter of 'build it, and they will come'." In addition to her acquired learning about how to build, host and update a website, Julie also had to get her head around the complicated, nebulous manner in which some sites rank higher than others on search engine result pages. **You know all**

those businesses listed on Page 2 of your Google search? Exactly.

"A lot of internet-based sales businesses like mine pay a lot of money to be on that first page of Google and Yahoo," she told me. "Perfect Rubber Mulch pays nothing. That is something I built through learning." I could tell by the tone of her voice that Julie Cole is immensely proud of this approach: rather than dropping thousands of dollars on buying ads and gaming her way to the top of Google, she took the patient route of establishing a solid name and reputation.

"When people look up 'rubber mulch' in their search engine, I want my name to pop up," she said. "I don't want to be a paid ad at the top, because they pay big bucks for those ads. I don't have an IT department. I don't have a marketing department. I have Julie – that's it. I can't pay a lot of money for ads, and make money at the same time, so I learned how to do what they do." **All at a cost any business can afford: zilch.**

Eventually, it paid off. In 2012, Perfect Rubber Mulch booked over one million dollars in sales – all off the back of one simple website that directs customers to call a nice woman in Ohio. The volume of calls has recently become too much for one person to handle; she now has a call center take inquiries, which Julie then follows up on directly. **The website itself is basically a Yellow Pages ad.** It's purely a **billboard** for her phone number: she doesn't have an online shopping cart, and doesn't capture her customers' credit card details.

The reason for this? Trust. "When somebody is buying something over the internet, the biggest problem they have is trust," Julie told me. Her sales can be huge – up to $20,000 per order, to sellers located as far away as South Korea. She has found that customers purchasing the kind of volume she operates in, spending the kind of money and organizing that type of logistics want to hear a human voice at the end of a phone line. They don't want to fill out a generic web form then push themselves through the natural hesitation and second-guessing that comes with the question of payment when there isn't someone making assurances directly to them on the other end.

Besides, if you're buying rubber ground-cover you're probably a risk-averse person to begin with.

Since her website is a call-to-action to get customers to call her, a lot of Perfect Rubber Mulch's success comes down to customer service. More specifically, it comes down to Julie. Warmth and friendliness on the phone plus – surprisingly – the simple act of promptly returning the calls of potential customers can be the difference between a customer for life and poisoning the well. "So many businesses fail miserably at returning phone calls," Julie said. She wasn't going to be one of those. **There's a reason they call it a phone "cradle" – that's where your business is born!**

Julie's astounding success with her online business only came after two previous attempts at offline entrepreneurship. The first was spurred by the boredom of a housewife whose youngest child had just started school. She had the idea of selling a catalogue named Just Gardens, which advertised handmade garden art. Julie's husband, a banker, loaned her $4,000 – with interest – to print the catalogue. "This was prior to the Internet becoming big in everybody's homes," she told me. "It was a miserable failure because, little did I know, everybody and their brother was going to come out with catalogues at that time: Wal-Mart and K-Mart started carrying garden art, too, all of it made in China."

Though Julie sold enough catalogues to exhaust her inventory, it was clear that Just Gardens was a dead-end business idea. It took her about a year to pay back her husband's loan, including the four percent interest. I asked her whether she resented her banker husband charging her interest on a personal loan. "No," she replied, much to my surprise. "It taught me a lesson: it taught me that you better know what you're doing before you attempt something. He treated me like one of his customers."

I can't emphasize this enough: Husbands, do not try that at home. Julie and her spouse are obviously trained professionals.

After her efforts with *Just Gardens* came interest from a couple of old ladies at Julie's church. They knew that she knew a lot about plants, and wondered whether they could hire Julie to landscape their home gardens. Her husband, Marty, told her to start thinking about selling her services, rather than products made by others. "Anybody can make money doing things," he said, "but your knowledge is valuable, and worth selling."

Marty's words struck me when I heard them. They reminded me a lot of Michael Grottola's story. He too had valuable knowledge worth selling. His was the result of decades of work experience and took some soul-searching to figure out. Julie's was the product of years of personal interest, and she was lucky enough to have Marty to point it out when her focus was elsewhere. But that is a distinction without a difference. **For both, their pot of gold wasn't at the end of some rainbow – it was right between their own ears.** We know how Michael's story goes, so what about Julie?

It turns out Marty Cole was right: Julie's landscaping business was a success. The breadth and depth of her knowledge paid immediate dividends. Her great rapport with her own gender helped too, as she found that women are the major buyers and decision-makers when it comes to landscaping matters. The business grew in lockstep with Julie's popularity in the area. Before long, she wasn't just doing sprawling suburban homes; she was tackling major corporate and commercial installations. One of those jobs—for a nearby indoor shopping mall—would prove fateful.

The storeowners were interested in a large beautiful seasonal display. Typically, Julie would design the display, bring in the plants and flowers, then on installation day lay down bark mulch to create a sense of a natural landscape. That wouldn't work this time, however. The smell of bark mulch indoors was going to be too much. **The mall's managers wanted customers to reach for their wallets, not plug their noses.** Of course, Julie Cole was up to the challenge. She had a few ideas and after a lot of research, a couple well-timed tips, and a number of phone calls, she found an old guy out in the country who was turning old car and truck tires into rubber pellets. The light bulb went on right away. She had her solution.

This was more than a way to keep one shopping mall from smelling like a squirrel's nest. It was the keys to the kingdom of personal and financial freedom. It set her down the path to discovering rubber mulch, founding a new online business for a niche market, and becoming a self-made internet millionaire.

What Julie Cole's husband told her about selling her knowledge certainly rings true for online marketer Ryan Deiss. "For somebody starting from scratch and looking to start an online business, I tell them that they have three options," he told me. "You can sell what you do online; you can sell what you make online; or you can sell what you know online."

And if you don't do anything, make anything or know anything, then you better be named Kardashian!

Ryan explained that the internet has turned the online labor market into a true meritocracy. By reducing the influence of petty interpersonal matters and interoffice politics, the internet job landscape is almost completely flat. "Stupid things like whether you like a person, whether they went to the right school; even the color of someone's skin, their religion, whether or not they speak with an accent – none of these things matter on the internet," he said. "It's 100 percent merit-based. If you continue to do a good job, you will get hired – if you want it."

Ryan Deiss is a digital marketer based in Austin, Texas who told me that he loves hiring people with more gray hair than him. As he said this, his eyes flicked up to my silver dome. I warmed to him immediately. Ryan is president of Idea Incubator, a company that covets the work-hard mentality and wisdom that generally comes with age. He despairs of the perception among employers that only young people have energy. It's a ridiculous generalization, he believes, because the youth don't stay young forever. Hell, they'll probably get married soon enough and start a family of their own, which will start to sap their energy and free time. These are the truisms that shortsighted employers forget when overlooking we so-called "empty nesters" whose children have left the home. **The only lunches we make are the ones we eat and we'll never go to another school concert as long as we live. How's that for "available?"**

Sell What You Do

For those looking to become masters of the virtual workplace, Ryan makes it clear to his clients from the outset that over-50s don't have to go out and start their own website, like Julie Cole did. They don't have to pore over web design textbooks, dress smartly to attend seminars via webcam, or pay a geeky teenager to code a site from scratch for them. In fact, it's usually much simpler than any of those options.

"There are already channels in place right now today on the web where you can sell what you do," he said, citing the example of TaskRabbit.com – a site that functions as a kind of electronic bulletin board, where users can post their services for sale, and people nearby can contact the poster directly to discuss the job and its conditions.

Men might advertise their lawn mowing skills, or offer to purchase and deliver groceries for time-poor folks; women might market their abilities at sewing, nanny services or assembling IKEA flat packs. "You don't have to be a master craftsman," Ryan told me. "It can just be 'busywork', because hey, maybe you have the time; maybe you just enjoy doing things that other people don't."

And who knows what you'll enjoy doing when there's someone paying you to do it?

Another example of a web-based services business that Ryan cited is Fiverr.com, where users can post things that they'd be willing to do for five dollars at a time. A quick scan of the website's front page shows people of all ages advertising business coaching services, hand-drawn sketches, personal fitness plans and video testimonials.

"You might be thinking, 'Why would I do something if I'm only getting paid $5.00?'" Ryan said. He'd read my mind. I couldn't remember the last time I'd done anything for five dollars. I was intrigued. He continued: "The reason is, you might do a small little task for $5.00 but then, if you do a good job for that person, they could hire you again and again and again. You might wind up getting some freelance work, which is another opportunity."

Online freelance marketplaces like Elance.com and oDesk.com are dominated by overseas workers willing to do writing and speaking related tasks, like interview transcribing, for ridiculously low fees. But Ryan told me that he – and many other American businesses – would much rather employee native English speakers based in the States.

Those with teaching backgrounds are perfect; if you were a language professor many moons ago, this is an ideal opportunity to earn some good money while working from home. Ryan has found people on Fiverr.com who did such a great job for five dollars that his company now employs them on retainer for up to $5,000 – $10,000 per month. **In other words, five dollars goes a lot farther than you might think.**

What skills do you have that you can post on TaskRabbit?

What can you do for $5 on Fiverr that will show you're worth $5k per month?

Check out Elance and oDesk. What are some of the things those overseas free-lancers offer that you can do better?

Sell What You Make

When it comes to selling what you make online, there's a great opportunity for over-50s to excel in this field, simply because those fine skills we learned in our younger years – from woodcraft to needlework to upholstery to hot sauce making. – are far less prevalent in the younger generations, who have grown up playing video games **while some poor kid in China makes their sneakers for them.**

Naturally, there are websites that cater to those who make unique products worth selling. "Etsy.com is one of the greatest websites in the world for people who like to make stuff," Ryan told me. In fact, their rules specify that only homemade products can be sold on the site. "You don't need your own website; you don't need your own merchant account. You just post it up there, Etsy sells it for you, and they cut you a check."

Imagine that: a post-industrial marketplace for pre-industrial crafting skills.

Another option that Ryan outlined is the little-known ability to create your own store on Amazon.com, and sell your products through their site. Wouldn't it impress the hell out of your friends if, at the next barbecue, you could proudly tell them about your beef jerky store on Amazon? I know I'd be impressed; I'd also be a customer. Or, if you want to launch your own store, Ryan described a site called Shopify that allows you to process orders through your own merchant account. It might be a little trickier and more tech-intensive, but Shopify also offers more flexibility and the ability to have greater control over the storefront. Shopify is the kind of place you go when you have a whole line of products and you have reached a comfort level with the Internet that someone like Julie Cole worked for a few years to develop.

Do you have a craft or hobby?

Have you ever made something that your friends say you could sell?

Go look at Etsy, Amazon and Shopify. Which feels more comfortable to you? **(Try not to buy too much!)**

Sell What You Know

Finally, Ryan told me about something that circled back to a point Julie's husband had made: selling what you know. It stands to reason that the longer you spend living on this planet, the more knowledge you accrue. My wife might disagree, but I certainly feel wiser with each passing day. If you've spent most of your career working for one company or corporation, then they've benefited immensely from the information contained in your brain. But now that you're on your own and looking for new opportunities, you might consider sharing that knowledge with other people – for the right price, of course.

Ryan mentioned a couple of websites that are based on this very principle: Udemy.com, and Skillshare.com, where people can create a training program in a specific area – business leadership, say – post it online and people buy it. This is ideal for those smart folks who, in their previous workplaces, were the go-to guy or gal for teaching the new employees about a particular aspect of the job – cake decorating in a bakery, for example. **It's like being a school teacher, with one major difference: Your students actually *want* to be there.**

One of the greatest changes that the Internet has brought to humanity is the ability to connect with other humans who share specific interests. **Yes, a lot of those people are creeps, getting to know other creeps, but not all of them!** There might only be a few hundred or thousand people in the world who want to know how to decorate cakes in a specific way, but if you could market that ability online and charge $500 a pop for the privilege of sharing what's in your brain with others, why wouldn't you?

Are you an expert in something?

Do you like to teach or coach or mentor?

Are you good at helping people solve problems?

If you do make cakes, will you send me one?

Keep in mind now, everything Ryan told me and everything Julie Cole did to get Perfect Rubber Mulch off the virtual ground doesn't just apply to people who got down-sized or lost a big chunk of their retirement savings in the Financial Crisis. These ideas work equally well for the Baby Boomers who need to make money now and those who want to make money because they have something to share, they don't want to be bored in retirement or they just want to stay sharp. **There are no bad times to make money. Only bad times not to have any!**

Regardless, I understand if all of this sounds incredibly daunting and overwhelming. It did to me at first as well. But don't worry--take a breath and read about what Ezra Firestone told me when I raised the very same objection. Coming to grips with these new websites and online processes sounds hard, I said to Ezra, who owns Smart Marketer Inc. and is an expert in using the Internet to build businesses. He replied that, once you overcome the fear and anxiety associated with learning these new technologies, it's really not too different from working offline.

"They just don't understand the technology," Firestone said of the baby boomer demographic, which comprises a significant proportion of his subscriber base. "So really, it's a question of first making sure that they understand it; from there, it's pretty similar. It's a matter of how do you go about picking a product to sell, marketing that product, and providing an experience that has people wanting to come back and do business with you again?

The technology barrier is what they're most afraid of, but it shouldn't be a big barrier to entry because there are a lot of platforms out there that have made it quite easy.

Besides, Baby Boomers *invented* personal computing. Shouldn't you be able to profit from it, too?

When Ezra said that, names like Shopify, Amazon, Fiverr and TaskRabbit cycled through my mind. Ryan Deiss certainly impressed upon me that the process of setting up an online store wasn't anywhere near as tough as I had imagined. Ezra agreed. It's not so much that the technology is difficult, he said; it's just a matter of building an initial awareness and familiarity.

The actual products that over-50s are selling online after receiving tutelage under his Brown Box Formula online marketing program are no different to the younger demographics he works with. "Some people are into dogs, so they sell dog stuff," he said. "Some people are into hobbies so they sell hobby stuff. It depends on what someone's interested in; their age demographic doesn't decipher what they sell."

No one needs to know your music-memorabilia business is run by the world's oldest Jay Z fan. Who would care, anyway?

The process Ezra outlined contains four steps: finding something that you want to sell, using a platform to sell that thing, marketing the product, and providing customer service. While anyone can fulfill these four criteria, Ezra believes that Baby Boomers tend to excel at the final step because, as a general rule, they treat people nicer.

It's a byproduct of the slower, more respectful times in which we were raised.

Who would have guessed that Boomers – the driving force behind Woodstock, free love and the 1968 Chicago Convention – would one day be prized for, of all things, their *good manners?*

"The boomer generation are the ones who reinvented themselves every decade of their lives," Ezra told me. "They're not going to be sitting on the porch in their 50s. They're out there doing things: learning to snowboard, becoming yoga instructors, and they're leveraging new technology. What I'm seeing is that boomers are not afraid of new technology; they're getting out there and doing it, and they're doing well." As I shook Ezra's hand, I was filled with optimism. I was half-tempted to quit writing this book and set up an online store of my own. Then I realized I already had one, on WilliamShatner.com ($1500 well spent if you ask me), filled with stuff I've made, memorabilia from things I did, and books that cover things I know. I guess I'd been following Ryan Deiss' advice all along without even knowing it.

As I discovered while speaking to these tech gurus, it's not always a matter of selling products online. Besides selling your skills or your knowledge, there's also an elusive fourth option: **selling other people's skills and knowledge. I'm talking about** building an online community that draws in a specific type of reader with unique content, which can then be leveraged to attract advertisers who would like nothing more than to build brand awareness within our coveted age demographic. This is exactly what Geri Brin, owner and publisher of a website called OverFifty, has been doing since 2010.

Though she is 66 years old at the time of our meeting in New York City, this is a woman with a lifetime of experience in the journalism and publishing business. Most of her career was spent at Fairchild Publications, working on trade and consumer magazines like Entrée for gourmet food stores, and Home Furnishings Daily, first as a journalist, then as an editor, and finally as a publisher – typically the highest-paying job in the business. **(Just ask Rupert Murdoch.)**

"I worked at a company that I gave my all at," Geri told me. "They were great to me. I worked hard, I rewarded them; they gave me money, they rewarded me." A tipping point arrived in the early 1990s though, when a trusted friend in the industry presented an opportunity: to make her editor and publisher of an entirely new custom magazine venture, potentially working outside of the Fairchild group. Management shut her down. Geri was beside herself with anger, but wasn't secure enough in her abilities and financial situation to tell her employer to stick it where the sun don't shine. B**esides, the sun was still shining on Geri.**

The industry friend hired another company and, years later at a social function, said to Geri that he didn't care whether Fairchild did the magazine; he coveted her expertise and contacts, and was looking to hire her. "'You could have done it on your own', he said to me. But I didn't. I was too oriented with the company. That was the first thing that made me realize I had to get out." She was married with two kids; her husband stayed at home, working on his art and writing. She was the breadwinner; the family depended on her.

So Geri stuck it out at her employer for a few more years, silently ruing the missed chance. "I was successful at what I did, and I loved what I did," she told me, "but I was afraid and didn't grasp an opportunity to take my passion and do it for myself, instead of somebody else." Yet the seed had been planted in her mind. If that guy was willing to hire her for her expertise, what was stopping her from throwing in the towel at Fairchild and hiring herself? **Or was her life like one of her magazines – covered on both sides and bound in the middle?**

A representative at a national retailer called Geri, asking her to create a 'magalog': a printed magazine that showed all of the retailer's items for sale, for wide distribution. Geri, thinking back to the last time this happened, asked whether they wanted Fairchild to publish the magazine. "She said, I don't care. We're asking you to do it," Geri told me. "I said to myself, 'Why am I going to stay and do this here, under the company, and give them the money I make?'"

There was only one thing standing in the way: **sheer terror.**

"When life isn't fulfilling and people want to do something else, a lot of them are not capable of figuring it out themselves so they have to talk to someone close to them that they trust to help them," Geri began explaining. "For me, that wasn't the case, but I was still scared, so I talked to my sister."

Her sister is a high-powered businesswoman six years younger than Geri. At a meeting in her company's big corporate boardroom, the elder sister nervously put her cards on the table. She laid out her vision for an independent online publication, but also her fears. What about a health plan? Geri had divorced her husband a few years earlier, which meant she couldn't just move over onto whatever **insurance** he had. And if she left Fairchild, she'd have to leave their health benefits too. **Sometimes, walking out the front door of a skyscraper can be scarier than jumping off the roof.**

Her sister looked at her and said three words: "Go for it."

They were the only words Geri needed to hear. With the emotional support of her business-savvy sis and a businessman 14 years her senior who Geri was seeing at the time, she took the plunge. In 1998, she started her own print publishing company, BrinSights LLC.

The business was quite successful, but midway through the **2000s**, the slow decline of print opportunities began to weigh on the minds of everyone in the industry. Digital publications were stealing away their audience and advertising dollars. Around the same time, Geri had an idea for her next project: she wanted to create something that celebrated the country's most fabulous older women. But she knew starting another magazine, like she'd done so often and expertly in the past, or turning the idea into a book, would be like digging a hole, filling it with tens of thousands of dollars and setting it all on fire. Advertisers were entranced by the seemingly limitless possibilities offered by the web, not by the same old dead-tree media they'd been booking for decades.

(I suppose now would be a good time to thank you for buying this particular dead tree. Thank you!)

"At that point, in 2008, I was Googling like crazy," Geri told me. "I was on the Internet constantly. I didn't have a Facebook page yet. I said to myself, 'I've got to start a website. More women in my generation are using the web; I've got to do it'." She picked a name—FabOverFifty.com—and sketched out a tagline that remains to this day: Where women of substance share their style. "I was going to do it for men too," she told me, "But I realized that, at the time, men [of my age] were not going to the web for advice about dressing and health."

With a lifetime spent working for publishing companies – first Fairchild, then her own business – Geri certainly knew how to produce beautiful magazine layouts. Why couldn't she take those skills and translate them from the printed page to a webpage? She had always worked closely with layout artists. The transition couldn't be that hard, she thought. And it wasn't. Suddenly, she found herself, at age 61, working with their digital equivalents: programmers who could bend the pages on FabOverFifty.com to match her every whim and desire. **While many people her age were considering a high-tech hip replacement, Geri gave herself a high-tech career replacement – and a hip one, too!**

Right at the beginning, Geri connected with upscale women's clothing stores all across the United States, asking them for their most desirable customers: the style influencers who set the tone for what ladies in the community were wearing. True to her journalism roots, Geri profiled each of those women on the website. These new stars were dotted right across the map, from Los Angeles and Dallas to

Chicago, Miami and New York. FabOverFifty.com wasn't beholden to geographic distribution like the printed publications of yesteryear; it could reach as far as the relationships, experience and wisdom Geri had developed over the years could take it.

At the heart of Geri's transformation from print princess to digital maven was her willingness to try new things; to go out on a limb and test how far she could stretch her knowledge in this new business environment and more difficult economy. "The 'new' part scares people, but it shouldn't," she told me. "What's there to be scared about? You're older; you've gone through so much in your life."

Hey, you survived the Nixon Administration. How much harder can anything be?

Geri's story reminded me of Julie Cole, the rubber mulch millionaire. Separated by 500 miles and wildly different backgrounds, the women are sisters-in-arms and digital pioneers for the Baby Boomer generation. Each woman saw an opportunity to embrace a new medium and grabbed it with both hands.

The internet didn't just shift the Information Age into warp drive, it created opportunities for people from all walks of life to take advantage of their skillsets and make as little or as much money as they want, spending as little or as much time as they have. I sell books and memorabilia on my personal website. I have a MadLibs-style poetry app in the App Store. They're not a major part of my business empire or annual revenue, so I don't spend a ton of time on this stuff, but people like what I'm doing and I like doing it. Julie Cole dove headfirst into the ever-changing world of web development and taught herself to build a website that she uses to juice sales for her at-home mulch business. **She has no overhead, no inventory, and no boss.** Early on she spent all her time focused on the web so today she can spend only as much as she needs to in order to return calls, fill orders and make hundreds of thousands of dollars. The rest of the time is committed to doting on her grandson. Geri pivoted from traditional print publishing to digital publishing and built an entire web-based platform that generates advertising and affiliate revenue. Her whole world is the Internet at this point, and she wouldn't have it any other way. **One woman's working to live, the other's living to work, but they're both workin' it.**

No matter where you fall on the spectrum, if you're thinking about the Internet as a part of the next productive phase of your life, make sure you are asking yourself the right questions. Some we've already covered, some are new—the product of ideas Ryan Deiss and Ezra Firestone talked to me about:

Do you do something really well?

Do you make something exceptional?

Are you an expert in a particular field?

How comfortable are you with the Internet?

How good do you want to get? Do you want to know how to do everything or do you just want something that is plug-and-play?

Do you need money or want money?

Is this a career or a side-business? A hobby, even?

The answers to these questions are important, as not all internet businesses are created equal. Some have a short shelf life with high immediate upside, others are longer-term propositions whose profit potential increases over time. For instance, the profit margins in Geri Brin's web publishing business aren't quite as high, or as quick in coming, as Julie's rubber mulch company.

You need to know where your business idea sits on that spectrum. You need to understand your personal and financial goals. You need to know your tolerance level for risk and the amount of work your idea requires. Are you more Team Julie or Team Geri? Me, I'm closer to Julie Cole, but that's just because I like to create and sell things.

That is not to take away from Geri's accomplishments. With minimal investment and maximum sweat equity, her website broke even in its third year of operation and now employs a full-time staff that manages a vibrant, engaged community of more than 250,000 unique visitors each month. I'm not really part of the target market, but I showed FabOverFifty.com to my wife, who has become such a fan of the site that on some days I can barely drag her away from the screen.

Manufacturers like FabOverFifty.com too. They are among the biggest advertisers on Geri's website: drug companies whose product is targeted at women going through menopause, for example. To these advertisers, FabOverFifty.com is a valuable lead-building resource to tap into the demographic of women around Geri's age. She mentioned that one of her advertisers sells sex education tapes for over-50s. "They're advertising with us and we're doing stories on couples who didn't have great sex lives, used their tapes, and now they are."

On second thought, maybe it's not so bad that my wife spends so much time on Geri's website after all.

CHAPTER FOUR

THERE'S NO BUSINESS LIKE A NEW BUSINESS: START-UPS AND INVENTIONS

Full Shatner Interview: CatchMeUp.com/Jeff & CatchMeUp.com/Brian

Jeff Frank has always had a mind for entrepreneurship. "I just like to do things differently. If you give me three choices, A, B, and C," he says, "I'll look for D, E, and F. That's just the way I've always done it." That's why, at 56, he decided to go into business for himself in what many considered to be a dying industry.

His 35-year career in the furniture industry started when Jeff took a job selling furniture for Woolco, the discount department store chain found by the Woolworth Company in 1962. **It was** the same year Sam Walton opened the first Walmart. Jeff is the first to admit that he wasn't a great salesman but, frankly, that wasn't really a problem. The

$199 living room sets sold themselves. What was a problem was that he couldn't sell pieces directly off the showroom floor. Here he was with decent merchandise priced to sell and customers ready to walk away with their newest impulse purchase, but the store's inventory was kept in a warehouse two states away in Pennsylvania. Even more frustrating, it required ample delivery time. All too often, this confluence of inconvenience was a deal-breaker for customers who were given a chance to catch their breath, step back and consider more fully their purchase decision. "Do we really need a new living room set?" they'd ask themselves. For many of them, **there just wasn't enough love for the loveseat.**

After three months of missing sales due to the lag time between purchase and delivery, Jeff had had enough. He hopped in his car and drove through the night straight to the warehouse and knocked on the door of the company president. The man wasn't expecting him — who would? — and he certainly didn't expect what happened next: the 21 year-old standing in front of him asked for a truckload of sofas.

"I could sell your stuff," Jeff told him. "I could sell a ton of your stuff if I had it available. But it's not. What are we going to do about this?"

What do you say to a kid **with that kind of stones?** Nothing, apparently.

The president sent a truck full of living room furniture straight away to Jeff's store in Washington, DC. That weekend, Jeff sold directly from the truck, which stayed parked behind the store. In three hours, the truck's entire contents were gone. Jeff's gumption was not.

A man who measures his sales in truckloads can rise through the ranks quickly, and Jeff did just that. Over the years he worked in nearly every role possible within the furniture industry. He was a sales manager, a buyer, and a government contractor. He worked in retail, in manufacturing, and he understood design. In each role his knowledge of the furniture business helped him excel and made him a lot of money as he exploited holes in the system he knew so well. "I've always looked for some other way to go about doing things that people haven't thought of before," Jeff admits. **He also found himself at the center of a growing circle of business relationships.** "I was able to bring in a lot of new business. Not only did I bring in the manufacturers, but I also got them the contracts." **He was turning cushions into cash**. A six-figure income arrived in short order.

Jeff's entrepreneurial spirit and his natural inclination to look for the holes in the system made him a standout in the field. His sense for the needs and the demands of the market kept him very well paid. His understanding of the product filled his head with new ideas and he had the expertise and **relationships** to capitalize on them. What he didn't have was control.

This point was driven home in the most painful way when his partner retired. Despite everything he'd given the company –

his passion, his brains, his moxie -- Jeff was fired from the firm by the man's son. What is it they say about no good deed?

But Jeff refused to let that insult become an injury. He knew his business and he knew his abilities. It was time to think big... by thinking small.

"There was a huge need for furniture that fits into small spaces, through narrow doors, narrow stairways, into RV's, into boats," he tells me. There was IKEA's flat pack product, of course—"knock-down furniture," as Jeff calls it—but no one was making a high-quality products that could easily fit through a small space. It was a huge need in the marketplace, so Jeff designed a totally new product to meet it. With the help of designer Glen Laughlin, he developed a line of high-end, ready to assemble furniture. It was as easily packaged and shipped as what IKEA was making but of a much higher quality. And perhaps more importantly, assembling Jeff's sofas wouldn't drive you insane.

Their prototypes, the designs for which Jeff patented, were so impressive that Jeff was easily able to sell the licensing rights to a huge manufacturer. The agreement would earn him a patent-royalty fee and a consulting fee for helping to develop additions to the line. Unfortunately, the manufacturer opted to sell the sofas for far less than their cost—obviously not a viable solution. They also did nothing to develop, improve, or expand the line. Despite being consistently paid a consulting fee, Jeff wasn't allowed in the factory.

None of his ideas **or** new designs were **ever** looked at. "They never changed a single thing in the three years they had it," Jeff says, "The pieces they had at the end of the three years were exactly the same as the ones they had before."

When the company went bust, its stock and licenses were acquired by another entrepreneur. This man didn't do anything with Jeff's designs either. Nor did he pay his bills.

This was getting ridiculous. Jeff had now been driven out from his position in the name of familial nepotism and watched as a **poorly run** manufacturer squandered **his best ideas. What was it going to take – starting his own damn furniture company?**

Well, OK then.

He went back to school to earn his MBA. Jeff had a clear plan and a great product. Surely things would now go his way. But his next obstacle wouldn't come in the form of outside forces. It happened inside his own chest: a massive heart attack. His recovery took months and **produced** a small mountain of medical bills. It was a financial setback that could not possibly have come at a worse time for someone trying to start a new business. Even worse, his health was now a **worry** for potential investors. They questioned it at every turn and used it to lowball him or pin him to unfavorable terms.

***He* survived the heart attack, but would his business?** Jeff was faced with two choices:

1.) Raise more money through investors and relinquish more control of his company

2.) Take on as little outside investment as possible and maintain control

The choice was clear for Jeff. **This company was** going to be his. It was the entire reason he had gone to business school. The most important thing was maintaining control of his company and the outcome of his product. He would find a way to work with what he had. **How many outside investors did he need, anyway?**

It turned out: just one. The investor brought the money and Jeff brought his design, expertise, and sweat equity to the table. In this way, Jeff would be able to minimize his financial risk but he would be investing his time and a lot of work. It was going to be a bootstrap operation.

It gets even better. If the mounting odds on the personal and financial sides weren't enough, the **entire American** furniture industry **was having a heart attack of its own.** As labor and manufacturing costs in the United States increased and raw materials became easier to source elsewhere, companies moved overseas. "Eighty percent of all wood furniture that is sold in this country is made overseas," warned Jeff. "It's that bad." The country was officially in a recession too.

"So there we are," says Jeff. "The recession has just hit, we have a product that is expensive furniture and is a type nobody's seen before. It's made by a small company that nobody's ever heard of, and our job is to convince people to buy this stuff."

Long odds – and Jeff wouldn't have it any other way. He'd built his company around a business model that required as little overhead cost as possible. That meant subcontracting all manufacturing and relying almost exclusively on reputation and word of mouth to get the company's name out into the market. It also meant going back to the drawing board.

With the help of Glen Laughlin, with whom he'd developed his initial ready-to-assemble prototypes, "we went back to work, and we came up with new designs and new patents," says Jeff. The two developed a line of furniture pieces meant to fit into small spaces and tight places. Sofas that could fit through narrow doors and up steep stairwells, into RV's and boats. Furniture that goes where no furniture has gone before. They called them Simplicity Sofas.

As if anything up to this point had been simple!

Building off of what he had learned from their previous efforts, Jeff and Glen approached their designs with a specific idea in mind. "I had learned that the best way to sell this thing and make money is to sell direct to consumers and not go through retail stores." This meant his pieces had to be easy to sell over the Internet and they had to be easy for his customers to assemble—easier than their first designs, easier than IKEA.

And they'd have another advantage, too. Thanks to his years in the furniture business, Jeff knew **its Achilles heel.** "In the furniture industry, customer service is terrible. We went exactly the opposite way." Jeff developed a customer service program founded upon communication first and foremost. Customers were notified of every step their furniture took in its development and shipping process. And their feedback was valued.

"Within 24 hours after the furniture arrives, we contact the customer," says Jeff. Something as simple as asking their customer: How did they like their new piece? Were they happy with the process? Does it look good in the room? **Easy questions, but questions no one else seemed to be asking.** And the ingenious design of the product allows Jeff to offer an even **harder-to-find** customer-service capability. If something does go wrong, it can be easily replaced at no charge. "We can replace just an arm if the arm is broken." No other furniture company would dream of free replacements, especially because doing so would likely mean replacing the entire piece. "The reason we can do it and nobody else can is because of the modularity of
the furniture," says Jeff.

Clearly, many customers were ready to replace their old way of buying furniture with Jeff's new approach. Simplicity Sofas began to gain traction in the market largely through word of mouth, which Jeff credits to his high quality product and excellent customer experience. They have grown so much, Jeff has already moved the manufacturing to a larger facility. Despite the challenges of scaling the business, the customer service has not suffered. "In six years and over 2,500 customers, we've never had a negative review," Jeff says proudly. Simplicity has been recognized as The Most Innovative Small Business in America and Jeff is finally beginning to take a salary.

But to get there, the kid who sold a truckload in an afternoon had to take a much longer view.

"Basically, it starts with a goal," he says, "When you have a goal, you just have to fix on that goal and go toward it. Sometimes it takes a lot of extra work to get there. You have to give up things to get there, but if you keep that goal in mind, just keep going and don't let anything in your way."

What makes Jeff Frank's story so **encouraging** is that it represents everything the Baby Boom generation has going for it:

Experience

Perseverance

Network

Work ethic

Service-orientation

Resources

And unlike many of today's generation, when Jeff faced adversity time and again, he did not roll over. He did not give up or point fingers. He took responsibility for his own fate. He learned from his mistakes, he marshaled his resources and experience, he talked to the people he knew, and he moved forward toward a goal of his own creation. In his mid-50s, on the other side of near-fatal heart attack, and the short end of the nepotistic stick (twice), **Jeff Frank didn't lie down on the couch — he reinvented it. By hiring himself**

"It's Time to Get Out" –Transitioning Technology

While Jeff Frank was repeatedly blindsided, Brian Hess could see the writing on the wall. It was just a matter of time until the larger cellular providers pushed his business, The Phone Works, out of the marketplace. He didn't care to wait around to watch it happen.

He knew the cellular industry through and through. He had to. Brian owned and operated what had been Columbus, Ohio's first retail cellular store and had been working in cellular since the technology began to take off. He understood the products, he understood the market, and he understood his customer base. **Most important, he understood the key to success in the cellular business: keeping your customers *your* customers.** He predicated his business model on customer service and a guarantee: your phone will work. **Even today that's a bold claim. Back in those days it was downright cavalier.**

"What I offered was something for your home, car, and business with awesome service," he told me, "We delivered. We guaranteed that the phone worked, and that was a rare thing."

And just like his phones, the business worked. At 37, Brian had paid back his investors and was sitting on $800,000 in profit. But he could feel competition breathing down his neck. As major cellular providers started opening their own stores to sell phones, his independent business became less viable. They controlled what Brian would never be able to: air time. And they could offer deals. "If you went to one of their stores after you were at one of my stores, I never saw you again."

Brian knew that it was time to get out. But where was he going to go? He liked the cellular business model: sell the phone and then continue to make recurring income through subscription service. He also understood that cellular technology had nowhere to go but up.

As he sat in his showroom, trying to come up with options, his eyes focused on the large box affixed to the wall.

His alarm system.

Brian knew nothing about alarms, outside of the fact that he had to pay a monthly bill for his service. **So he did what any curious electronics entrepreneur would do: he broke into it.** "Inside, I saw this really dinky, worthless battery," he says. There wasn't much else inside the big, metal alarm panel so Brian couldn't help but wonder, "Why the big box?"

He could see no reason why he couldn't "go get a CD player and gut it and put those parts inside." Rather than risk a minor electrical fire, he teamed up with an engineer to outfit the alarm in a much smaller vessel and make it work on a phone line. They then set about to take the alarm in another direction; one that Brian had seen an increasing demand for in the phone business. **He wanted to cut the cord** — to utilize cellular technology to make it portable.

The alarm business had been around a long time. Cellular had been around long enough. But no one had found a way to combine the two. To create a wireless alarm panel—one that didn't need to be tethered to a wall—would actually upgrade the security of the system. With the wall unit, an intruder could disable the system by simply unplugging it from the phone line. "So, silly me with the old portable cellular business," says Brian, "I thought, 'Well, I'll make a portable alarm system!'"

And just like that, Brain cut the cord to his old business,

kicking off a years-long process of invention, re-invention, and refinement as Brian honed his Tattletale alarm system. As with Jeff and Simplicity Sofas, Brian **hated junk,** and was steadfastly dedicated to building the highest quality product. So much so, that he gave up the opportunity to work with the country's largest alarm manufacturer after the company told him he needed to compromise his design. Instead Brian **spend $100,000 developing his prototype and** took it to Cadex, a small company out in Texas that promised to give him exactly what he wanted. Brian attributes this perfectionist drive to the values with which he was raised: if he's going to do something, he's going to do it the right way.

Hadn't anyone told him that's not how people do things anymore?

Eight-hundred thousand dollars of his own money later, Brian was holding what he refers to as "The Best-Built Stupid Box." His prototype finally matched the vision he had many years before. "It was supersonic," he describes, "It sent a signal out in 6/10ths of a second and the sensors could go half a mile." His system was equipped with a built-in motion detector, strobe lights, siren, 15 hours of battery backup, and three watts of cellular power. It was light years ahead of anything else on the market. But just as it seemed that Brian's years of hard work were about to pay off, two words brought his progress to a crashing halt.

"Ice chest."

An acquaintance came into Brian's shop. The man had followed his inventive process over the years and was familiar with Brian's prototype. And he'd found a flaw.

"Hey, I know how to beat your alarm."

Brian smiled. "All right. What do you have?"

"I'm going to come in and I'm going to bring in a Coleman cooler full of ice water," he said. "I'm going to drown your system in an ice chest."

He was right. **Brian had packed his invention with a bounty of the latest wireless technology, but he hadn't taught it to swim.** All alarm systems allow a 40-second window between engagements—someone walks in the house—and activation. This window gives the homeowner time to punch in the code to turn it off. In that 40 seconds, the alarm is doing nothing and the system, which is sitting out in the open, is completely vulnerable. Of course, Brian could make the panel waterproof but the underlying problem, the 40 seconds of vulnerability, would still be there. In his mind, there was only one decision.

"I'm not going to market with this."

Brian called the president of the manufacturing company with his bad news. In spite of the **flaw**, the man was still resistant to the idea of postponing production and sale.

"Brian, it's still the best portable alarm system I've ever seen!"

So what? It was Brian's prototype. And he wasn't going to put it out into the world until it was perfect, until it was made right. It was the same ethical approach that he had with his phone business and it was holding true now. Brian wasn't about to build a slipshod product;

he wasn't looking to milk the market. "There's no 50-50. You have to be 100% in," Brian explains. "That's the way my dad raised me."

Much to the grief of would-be burglars the world over. But I'm getting ahead of myself.

Because now a new question plagued Brian: "How do you make that box know it's in a fight?" It took six months to solve the problem but Brian was able to configure Tattletale to instantly trigger the alarm if it is tampered with during those first 40 seconds. Finally, it was ready. His alarm system went to market.

The invention process is a difficult one even for the guy tinkering in his garage. I've had any number of ideas over the years, some I've done patent searches on only to find they already existed, others I've taken all the way to the prototype phase before realizing there was no real market for them. It can be a tough pill to swallow. Add in the need for funding and the stress factor can climb exponentially. **You realize pretty quickly that thinking up an idea the world has never seen before is actually the *easy* part.**

Brian had invested two years and $800,000 of his own money into the development and manufacture of his Tattletale system. He had also just raised one million dollars from investors by selling 18% of his company and cashing in on his industry credibility—something that would be nearly impossible for someone 20 years his junior. "They buy who you are and where you've been," he points out. Brian had been a top-selling cellular dealer for ten years. His years of success spoke well of him and demonstrated his knowledge of the technology. Still, as he proposed entering a new industry with a new invention their question was, as it always was, "Can you pull this off?"

Brian had raised the stakes on everyone by telling his manufacturer, "I'm not going to market until I have this right." Now, all-in, having assumed major personal financial risk himself, it was going to be an even harder thing to tell "a million-dollar bunch of investors… it's not selling."

But that's what happened. When Tattletale finally hit the market it quickly became apparent that Brian's worst-case scenario was coming true: his product wasn't selling and he was running out of money.

Buy why? The box was perfect!

The Tattletale system is a sizable black box made of molded hard plastic, with a slightly futuristic shape and a foreboding look to it. Perfect to give intruders a second thought, right? The problem is, intruders don't buy alarm systems. Homeowners do, specifically wives and mothers. Well, women didn't like the look of the Tattletale system. "We couldn't get women to let it in the house. They wanted to put it in the closet, or in the basement."

The box could finally swim. But it wouldn't fly.

The cost of the alarm was proving prohibitive as well. Its technology outpaced anything else in the industry and the price reflected that. Brian was charging $899 for the box while his competition was charging $99. Neither the design, nor the cost, could be significantly altered. Brian was staring down the barrel of failure and at a lot of unhappy investors. The prospect of having to start all over again was a very real thing, and the clock was ticking.

Brian was down to $32,000 in payroll money. Realistically, Tattletale could last one more month. It was like being on the Enterprise — **"I'm givin' ya' all she's got, Captain!"** — except the Enterprise was pretend. Brian was looking at a **very real** empty refrigerator.

Then, just like that, Brian sold 1,000 units. But it wasn't housewives who bought them. It was hardhats: a million-dollar sale to a **construction** company that planned to use his units in the trailers on their job sites. "Terrific. My box is trailer trash," he joked. His ego may have been bruised, but Brian **wasn't about to spit at a million in revenue.** He went home, licked his wounds, and came back the next day with a new focus.

"This is a guy's box. That's how it's going down, and it's not going to change." He began to market the Tattletale system specifically for job sites and developed new ways to tailor the system to the needs of that market. He pioneered outdoor wireless technology; motion detectors, sensors, and on-demand tracking that make it impossible to steal a Bobcat.

It turns out the box had been right all along. It was the target market that was wrong.

Brian has since earned back all of the money he staked in his venture and, with Tattletale earning $5 million a year in sales, his investors are very happy. "I have a brand that's never been defeated and not one dissatisfied customer in 15 years."

Just a lot of dissatisfied thieves.

Brian credits his success to his 100% dedication. "You've got to put your butt on the line," he says, "If you are not authentically in, don't be in." But there's more than just dedication at the heart of Brian Hess's story, there's something more of which dedication is just a part; something kind of unique to his—and our—generation: **strong values.**

Throughout his early years in the cellular industry and then bringing the Tattletale system to fruition, his values anchored his success. Just look at what he's talked about in our conversations:

Being "authentically in" – that's called **honesty**

Putting "your butt on the line" – that's called **sacrifice**

"There's no 50-50" – that's **dedication**

Delivering "awesome service...guaranteed" – that's **humility**

Doing something "the right way" – that's **integrity**

The values exhibited by both Brian Hess and Jeff Frank are what make the two men as successful as they are today in the face of all they have endured. Theirs are traits most of us over-50s can recognize in ourselves, our generation, and the culture that defined us.

Unless you're still a hippie, in which case: Get a job!

But what makes Brian Hess and Jeff Frank successful as entrepreneurs is that they leveraged decades of experience inside specific industries (they didn't throw them away or discount them) and used that knowledge to identify unfulfilled needs and fill them; to spot opportunities and take advantage of them.

This is something each and every one of you who have worked your entire lives at one company or in one industry could do today.

You start by asking the right questions:

What could they be doing better in my company/industry?

What ideas have I had to make things easier or more efficient?

What would I change if I were in charge? How would I do it?

Who do I know who thinks like I do?

What institutional/industry knowledge do I have that younger/newer people don't?

I asked myself a version of these questions when the Internet really started to explode and TV was having trouble figuring out what to do about it or how to take advantage. Applying the lessons from my decades in the entertainment industry is why I ended up doing the Priceline commercials and taking the stock-option compensation deal they offered that netted me millions. It's why I've had a personal website for years where you can follow my appearances, contact me for booking, or buy memorabilia. It's why I am able to do Brown Bag Wine Tasting on my YouTube channel without a second thought or a care in the world.

So what's your Simplicity Sofa? Your Tattletale system? Your Brown Bag Wine Tasting? I know you have one. Spend the time to figure it out. The world is waiting and only you can do it.

CHAPTER FIVE

PAYING THE COST TO BE THE BOSS: BUYING INTO A FRANCHISE

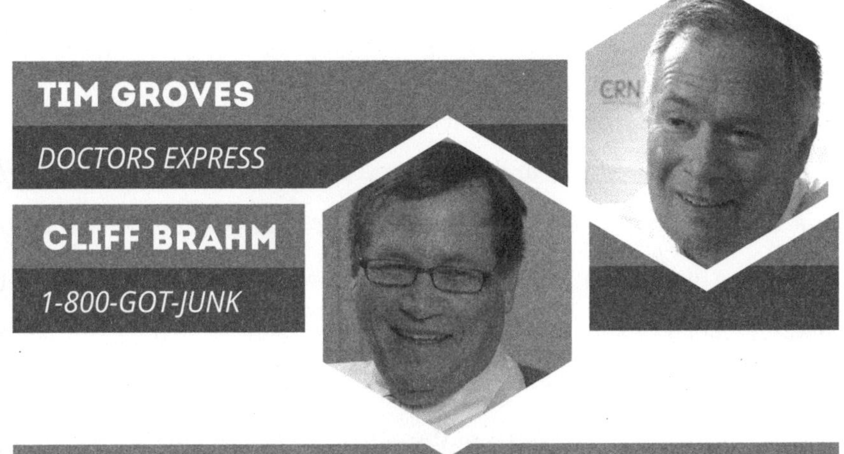

Full Shatner Interview: CatchMeUp.com/Tim & CatchMeUp.com/Cliff

In 1964, CBS rejected Gene Roddenberry's Star Trek concept in favor of a show called Lost in Space by Irwin Allen. Science fiction was big back in the mid-'60s and Allen had not only produced a number of popular sci-fi films in the late '50s and early '60s, but had already adapted one of them successfully—Voyage to the Bottom of the Sea—earlier that year for ABC. Gene Roddenberry on the other hand, while an avid science fiction fan himself, was best known around town as a writer for shows about cops, cowboys or soldiers. At the time, rejecting Star Trek was a smart move for CBS.

Gene then took the concept to NBC, who bought it and had the pilot in production by the end of that same year. It starred a wonderful actor named Jeffrey Hunter in the lead role of Captain Christopher Pike. The network passed on it in early 1965, but took the unusual step of paying Gene to write a second pilot—the first one was "too intellectual"—and thank goodness for that, because Captain Kirk didn't exist until that script. NBC liked this pilot episode—called "Where No Man Has Gone Before"—and premiered the show in the fall of 1966. The show ran two more seasons before our luck ran out in February 1969, shortly after we finished filming Season 3. All told, we lasted 79 episodes.

By all measures, Star Trek should have faded into obscurity after our cancellation like most of the other science fiction shows from the period: Lost in Space, Voyage to the Bottom of the Sea, Time Tunnel, Land of Giants. Our show was different though. In the 45 years since the original series went off the air, Star Trek has spawned five spin-off series, twelve feature films, more than 75 computer and video games, at least 500 separate novels, a Sears catalog worth of merchandise and an entire convention circuit. It is, as they say, a cottage industry. I don't know why we were different than those other shows; I don't know why we developed such a loyal fan base, but why is not the point of this story. The point is to illustrate the power of a franchise.

If there is one person who understands the power and value of a franchise, you're looking at him. **(OK -- reading him.)** Besides starring in all 79 of the original Star Trek episodes, I went on to voice my character in the animated series a few years later, appear in eight of the twelve films—one of which I directed—and co-write 11 of the Star Trek-themed books. In a very real sense, the Star Trek franchise made my career and everyone else's in the regular cast. The irony is, this was an understanding I came to, and appreciated, only later in life. At the time, it didn't feel like Star Trek made us, it felt like we made Star Trek.

With the exception of James Doohan (Scotty) and DeForest Kelley (Bones), the rest of us were in our late 20s and early 30s when NBC picked up the show. We'd all guest starred on a number of popular (and not so popular) shows in the years leading up to that first season, but none of us had experienced our big break. We had no idea if this would be it, but we knew it was a risk. NBC had something like 24 pilots ordered that season and while sci-fi was indeed popular at the time, no one had the first clue which shows would make it. In '64, the year NBC bought the show, CBS canceled *The Twilight Zone.* The next year, ABC canceled Jonny Quest and Outer Limits after one and two seasons, respectively. Anything was possible, **and most of it was bad.**

NBC brought us to air with a modest 17-episode run. We had great ratings with young viewers and decent reviews from the critics, but we didn't gain as much traction with a broader audience as the network had hoped, which put us on the chopping block almost immediately. **Whatever peril the *Enterprise* may have found herself in each week was nothing compared to the vicious universe of**

network TV. Before the end of the first season, the network ordered a dozen more episodes and renewed us, but put us on at 8:30 on Friday nights for that second season. **There went those young viewers I just mentioned.** Not that I blame them. What would you have rather been doing on a Friday night when you were a teenager: watching TV or going out? **(And that was back when music was still good.)** Still, we managed to survive budget cuts, scheduling changes and an aborted cancellation for another season—thanks to our small, but dedicated fan base—before NBC finally pulled the plug.

All of this is to say that work on the original series was not all **tribbles and hot, green women.** It was hard work with an uncertain future. Being in the middle of it, helping carve a new path for science fiction television, I did not see all the opportunities *Star Trek* was creating—that required a little hindsight and a lot of distance—but they started to spring up almost right away. We went directly into syndication despite having fewer episodes than most studios require; within a couple years, a number of different games came out and novels began to get published. The animated series was launched in 1973 and by the middle of 1975 Paramount had paid Gene Roddenberry mid-7 figures to write the first feature motion picture script. In less than a decade, Star Trek had become a franchise.

What made the *Star Trek* franchise so powerful to me as an actor and so valuable to the creators who owned it, was that each successive Star Trek endeavor was proportionately less risky because it was built on the success of everything that came before it. No one had to reinvent **the warp drive, so to speak.** No one had to spend the time or money to create an entirely new universe. All we had to do was honor the universe that Gene and the original cast had created, live by its laws, do something new and fun within the broad confines of that universe, and we were more likely than not to succeed.

This is the essence of the franchise model: **giving people more of a good thing.** And it is a great option for anyone looking to go into business for themselves without the risk of starting completely from scratch. It begs the question though: what exactly is a franchise?

There are three types:

Licensing franchises – these are like sports teams and beverage companies where the parent company offers up a license to use their branding and trademark in association with the franchise's normal business operations. **If you can make and sell New York Yankees hats without getting arrested, you've got a licensing franchise.**

Distributorship franchises – think of car dealerships and gas stations, where the main company lets you set up shop and sell their products in your region. You can make a lot of money this way if you're good. That's why most people who own distributorships don't just own one place, they own several.

Business Format franchises – this is the kind of franchise that most people think of when someone talks about owning a franchise. McDonalds, Subway, 7-11, Oil Changers, etc. You pay them an initial start-up fee and a cut of your profits every month and in exchange they basically give a successful business-in-a-box with a proven model, an established brand name, and a battle-tested operating system.

We'll focus here on the last of these three — business format franchises — because they provide the quickest and surest path to small business success for those of us over 50. **They especially appeal to folks** who are tired of the rat race like Thomas Betts and Dave Bateman were, but don't have quite the same appetite for risk. **They're** also ideal for people who have previously thrived inside corporate systems but are now interested in doing their own thing and being their own boss in the next phase of their lives. **It's a way to be both corporate *and* independent at the same time.**

That's how Tim Groves put it to me when we sat down to discuss the opening of his newest Doctors Express clinic in Greenville, South Carolina. The idea behind Doctors Express is simple: an urgent care business without the hospital or the long emergency room waits. What makes the idea novel, though, is that each Doctors Express is placed in a retail setting; essentially a storefront like a Starbucks or a **Baskin Robbins. But instead of selling treats, they sell treatment.**

"Everyone needs a doctor at some point," Tim explained, "so why not design a clinic that fits their needs and lifestyle. Everyone wants everything quick, convenient, inexpensive these days, so we put Doctors Express clinics where you're going to be doing different kinds of errands anyway."

Besides the obvious benefits of ease and convenience, what makes this concept work so well is that it allows the doctors to focus on the medicine and the franchise owners to focus on the business.

No one wants their doctor worrying about whether he bought enough printer toner to make it through the week. And guess what: Doctors don't want to think about it either!

"A lot of them coming out of school, or even established doctors, have a hard time seeing patients and trying to manage a business on top of it," Tim told me. "This way our doctors see patients all day and I take care of the investment of actually building out the office."

"So does this make the doctor your employee then?" I asked. I've met a lot of doctors in my day and I didn't think many would ever consider themselves employees.

"Yes and no," Tim said. "In my case our lead physician is also my partner. It's like a joint venture. But we have three other doctors that work just on an hourly basis. A lot of doctors do this actually."

I stand corrected. But what was most surprising to me was not that doctors would be employees, rather it was that before Tim had even jumped into the franchise game he'd already analyzed the risks and taken the path he was more comfortable with. He could have dived in headfirst, owned 100% of that initial franchise and made everyone his employee. If he wanted to be his own boss and do his own thing, what better way than owning it all? With 100% of the ownership, of course, he would bear 100% of the risk for its failure. In his mid-50s when he opened the first Doctors Express, that gamble was a bridge too far. By taking on a partner, he could mitigate the risk and avoid over-extending himself financially. **And** by taking on a partner who was a doctor, he also found someone who could fulfill the services that were the entire mission of the business. **Better to own half of a thriving success than a hundred percent of a goose egg.**

These initial business decisions by Tim reminded me very much of the questions Michael Grottola and Thomas Betts asked themselves when they prepared to take their first next steps: What are you good at? What assets do you have that you can leverage? What kind of risks are you really willing to take? **Because Tim had a lot to lose.**

After 23 successful years in the hotel industry, Tim was sitting at the top of the proverbial food chain. He was a high-ranking executive with Extended Stay hotels, in charge of sales and marketing for 686 properties around the country. During his tenure he had successfully grown the company to three times its original size. There was plenty to be proud of, but it all felt rather empty to Tim and he couldn't articulate why that was. It was a good job. The money was there. His employers encouraged autonomy, instead of treating him like a cog in a wheel. As Tim told me, "They always told you to think like you owned the business. Think like an owner." They, in effect, told him to be his own boss.

Over time, Tim got in the habit of doing that. He weighed each of his decisions carefully, considering their impact on the bottom line as if it were his bottom line. He expertly rode out the highs and lows of the hotel business, which runs in cycles tethered to the economy, with the big picture always in mind. He made personal sacrifices to benefit the company. He had already uprooted his family from L.A. to Atlanta, to Greenville, South Carolina and travelled constantly to visit hotels sites and regional offices. It's what he would have done if the business were his. His mindset and his work ethic had brought him a lot of success but little fulfillment.

**(And let's be clear: Telling employees to think like owners is, at heart, a crummy move. Will you be paying them like owners if their ideas and hard work bear fruit? No?
Then don't confuse things.)**

Finally, after years of thinking like an owner, Tim wanted to start living like one: "I could own my own business and be able to do things completely the way I want." Maybe that was his answer.

"I really would like to be owner."

But an owner of what? Nothing leapt out at him. **All he was sure of was that he was ready to check out of the hotel business.** The **hospitality industry** runs with the same cycle as the economy, riding high when the market is up and bottoming out when the market is low. And, as the man in charge of sales, Tim lived and died with it. The stress had already taken a toll on him and now, in 2007, with the country heading into recession, the market looked bleak. This alone would have brought enough pressure to bear on his job, but his company had just been sold and new owners brought a new set of expectations. High expectations. Extended Stay hotels had just been purchased at its peak **but it was about to hit a down wave. Tim wasn't a surfer; he didn't look forward to that ride.**

"No matter how great you were, when things are going down and the revenue is going down, they're going to look at the guy who is responsible for revenue." Tim realized that this might be his opportunity to get out while the getting was good. So he began to weigh his options.

He wasn't looking to start over, to switch industries and claw his way into the C-suite again over the next decade. He wanted to build something that would be his. He realized: "I want to be able to have something that I grow, that I personally own." He knew how to grow a business and he knew how to keep customers happy with great hospitality, but still he didn't know what that business would be — **only that it wouldn't have anything to do with hotels. So what opportunity did he jump to?**

Nothing. Tim left his job with no set plan to do anything but unwind and spend time with his family. It was a decision he needed to make for himself. When the time was right, he would chart his new course. **As Paul Newman famously said, "Sometimes nothing can be a pretty cool hand."**

After a couple months, Tim was fully rested and e**ven more thoroughly** bored. It was time to get back to work, this time as his own boss. **He was so bored, he even started reconsidering his former industry.** "I could do a hotel consulting business," he thought, "I know a lot about sales and marketing, and they're always looking for new ways to drive revenue into these businesses." It made sense. A consulting business would allow him to grow his own business while putting his decades of experience and Rolodex of connections to good use. It seemed to promise a fresh start without having to start over.

But was it really the fresh start he needed? Consulting would require extensive travel that would steal time away from his growing daughters. He would be a one-man show as all responsibility fell on him. Tim realized, "I'll be right back on the road again, and all the business will be between my ears. I'll probably be just swamped with all kinds of stuff going on." It also meant returning to the industry that had burned him out. And there was the recession to think about: the highs would not be as high and the lows would be lower. Even as a consultant, he would have to ride the cycles of the hospitality industry and he had no interest in doing that.

Maybe that would have to be his starting point: He wanted to work in an industry that was *always* in demand.

Tim took advantage of seeing a career counselor—paid for as a provision of his departure package. He wanted to use the service as a sounding board, someone to bounce his ideas against to see if anything stuck. It was like therapy, **without the box of tissues.** And it produced a **fateful question:**

"Have you ever thought about buying a franchise?"

Tim sat back **in the chair at** his career counselor's office. "Not really."

As in, not *ever*. Tim had literally never thought about it for a second.

"There's a guy who does these seminars who explains how it all works. It would be a great opportunity to learn more about it. Then, if you're interested, he'll meet with you and discuss what your revenue goals are, how much you're willing to invest, and what you're good at. He can even match you up with franchises that might be a good fit."

"There are people that do that?"

"There are."

There was even a seminar coming up soon.

Would Tim like to go?

"Sure."

Tim's knowledge of franchises was minimal. He knew Marriott offered franchises, he had eaten at Subway before, and the basic idea appealed to him. The things he needed to get his business off the ground would be provided; everything else was up to him. **So he went to the** seminar and began to explore his options.

You might say that the idea had set up a franchise in Tim's head. With the help of his broker, Tim quickly whittled down the options. Patio screens didn't interest him at all. The food and beverage market seemed rich, but he saw a problem there, too.

"I thought about having a fast food franchise for a second," Tim told me, "They're great but there's one on every corner. I just thought food and beverage is so competitive. I'm still amazed that more of them open all the time." Entering into a highly competitive field exceeded the risk level that Tim was willing to take on.

He kept flipping through brochures. Starbucks. Transworld Business Advisors. Doctors Express... He almost tossed the information aside with the others. "The first thing I thought was, 'Medical, I don't want to have anything to do with it because I don't know anything about it.' But then Tim started looking at it a little bit more. Sure, he didn't know anything about the medical industry, but his skills fit the company and the company fit his desired lifestyle. **He took it seriously enough to fly to the** company's headquarters in Baltimore to meet with the leadership.

(Luckily, he was still willing to stay in a hotel.)

The idea behind Doctor's Express made sense to him. It was a familiar concept done in an entire new way. "Urgent care is not a new thing but still, a lot of people don't know about it. It's meant to be in between a primary care position and the emergency room." Doctors Express promised to make urgent care even more convenient, accessible, and inexpensive. **By now** Tim **was nearly sold.** "Everyone needs a doctor at some point," and here was a service that could cater to that need while making it easier to get to. Best of all, he didn't need a medical **background**. His role would be to manage and grow the business and let the doctor's manage their patients. His background was a perfect match for the demands of the business. **Best of all**, he could bring with him something that was sorely lacking in the medical industry.

Hospitality.

"We try to provide great hospitality skills to our staff. When someone comes in, they get treated like they're checking into a hotel. We smile, we greet them, we give them great service, and we try to give them great service all the way through." A doctor's office **that's pleasant to visit?** Now that is rare. **And Tim knew it was a great way to set Doctor's Express apart.**

He had found his franchise.

Still, it wouldn't come without risk. Tim's store would be number 15 in the country and the first of its kind in Greenville, SC. This presented a challenge in terms of getting his name out there, but it also meant that he wouldn't have much competition. Doctors Express also guaranteed him a population radius of 50,000; a nice wide market. And the barrier to entry was a high one—"It's not cheap to buy all this equipment and build all these things out"— so there wasn't going to be another Doctors Express opening up immediately. And if another Doctors Express did eventually open in Greenville, it would bring the opportunity for collaboration, to share costs and make life easier for both owners. Yes there were risks, but they were mitigated. Tim **pulled the trigger.**

The Doctors Express franchise model made it as easy as possible for Tim to start putting his storefront together. He didn't need to understand the ins and outs of x-ray equipment because the homework had been done for him and a discount rate had already been negotiated. He had even been given a proven business plan. As Tim explained, "They give you a template, 'Here are all the vendors. Here's who you get your x-ray from. Here's who you get your supplies from.' They negotiate volume discounts so you don't have to recreate the wheel on every single aspect of your business."

You've got to love the franchise model. How else could a burnt-out hotel executive in his mid-50s build a state-of-the-art medical facility?

Still, all that **corporate help couldn't spare him** from a steep learning curve and the terrifying moments that so often come with entrepreneurship. **For Tim, one of them came soon after he opened his doors. And it came in the form of one thought**: "Uh oh."

Everything was in place. The office was staffed. There were even appointments in the books. But the company still wasn't online with every insurance network. The process had taken much longer than he ever expected. The problem was that none of the insurance companies knew who he was. This was the one thing Doctors Express couldn't pre-arrange for Tim because insurance coverage varies on a state-by-state basis. And it was taking too long to move through the process. "There was a lag time between when we opened and we were accepted on all that," Tim said.

So, for many patients, the only money Doctors Express could collect was the co-pay the patients themselves forked over — a tiny fraction of the true cost of the visit. Financially it was a terrible business proposition. But that's when Tim's hospitality background, his insistence that every patient enjoy a positive experience, kicked in.

"We just said, 'We want to make a friend out of these people, so we'll take them.' If we aren't accepted with that insurance, we'll just take them for their co-pay, treat them for $20, and make them feel great about it so that they'll come back later." His customers were treated well and left happy, hopefully to tell their friends about their positive experience. **His background in an entirely different indus-**

try was serving him well.

In the meantime, Tim was writing checks out of his personal account to cover payroll, rent, and to keep the lights on. "All that stuff entrepreneurs do when they start out," he says while shaking his head. "You think, 'Well, this is fun.' **Tim took another page from his hotel experience and created** direct mail and Internet marketing campaigns to grow business while anxiously hoping to get past the red tape. Postcards had been sent, ads had been placed, and word of mouth was spreading, but would it turn around fast enough?

On one of many sleepless nights, Tim turned to his wife and asked, "Have I lost my mind? Did I make the biggest mistake of my life?"

His wife sighed, "I'm not sure. I'm not divorcing you yet."

That was a relief.

It took about a year to get the growth arrow going up and to the right. In fact, it turned around so **fast** that Tim is planning to open a second Doctors Express franchise. It will be the third storefront in the Greenville area. Marketing costs are shared among all three, which makes the startup cost of Tim's second franchise considerably lower.

"We're doing pretty well now. That's why I'm doing a second one. I've certainly made a lot of mistakes. Now that I've gotten it in my mind, I've perfected it to a degree: how to open these things and how to get it going faster, I'm a lot more confident in opening the second one. I feel it's going to do well financially."

Why wouldn't it? It's a business in a box, and he'd already

torn one box open.

Like Thomas Betts, Tim had burned out. Like Michael Grottola, he had decades of experience in one industry that he could leverage into another. Like Dave Bateman, he had relocated looking for something more. Like Geri Brin and Julie Cole, he used the Internet as a platform and a tool to build his new business. **And it all started** inside the comfort of an **executive** suite he didn't have to leave.

That last part probably sounds funny to the subject of our next story. Cliff Brahm didn't have the luxury of picking his exit date. The company picked it for him. I'll let his wife explain.

"Downsized?"

Her disbelief echoed Cliff's own. This wasn't a conversation Cliff had expected to have that afternoon. Cliff was shocked; shaken at his core. He had called home to break the bad news as gently as he could.

"I can't believe they would do that," his wife said. "What are we going to do?"

Good question. Luckily they didn't have to decide that day. His company had given him a good severance package and a promise to help him transition.

"We'll find a way through this. We have a severance, and we'll find the next great step."

In the days that followed, Cliff tried to figure out what that next great step would be. He was great at his old job in retail merchandising, had built out a strong network of connections over the years and an even stronger reputation. In a matter of weeks, he had received an enticing offer to move into a VP role at a new company. Cliff excitedly flew out to meet his potential new employers. "God, this is going to be great," he thought, "I'll be back working again, it's an industry I know, I have a lot of connections, and it's perfect." The visit went well—"I was so pumped"—and Cliff flew back to Cincinnati ready to prep his family to move to Charlotte. **But then, thirty thousand feet above Kentucky, something started to feel not-quite-right.**

"I just didn't want to get back into the rat race. After being in it for 49 years, in many different positions, higher level, lower level, I don't want to be in this boat again." He wanted to make decisions for himself. He never wanted to worry that someday his boss would come through the door and say, "Thanks for your time but we're moving in a different direction." Cliff wanted to build equity in something that would be his, to be the decision maker. "I wanted to control my own destiny."

He was literally up in the air.

By the time he landed, Cliff knew he couldn't accept the offer. The decision scared him, of course, but it made him optimistic too. With the full support of his wife, Cliff planned to open his own business. Unlike Tim, Cliff was not seeking to leave the industry he had come from. "I could do the same business. I had a lot of success and I had people lined up that wanted to jump on board with me, from a sales and an operational standpoint." He was going to take his expertise and put them to work for himself. Cliff started putting together a business plan for his own retail merchandising business.

Cliff built out a plan for his start-up, a ground to nation-wide business that could grow quickly. He just needed the money—$400,000 to get started. He chose to go the small-business-loan route at his regional bank. The bank chose to go the "we're not going to fund it" route. They deemed it too risky given the recessive economic climate. Cliff was back at square one.

Was the plane's cabin low on oxygen when he made this decision? No matter; it was too late to second guess himself.

Undeterred, Cliff set his sights on options that carried lower risk. "I can't get a loan at the bank," he thought, "I'll go to an established business, like a franchise." He made his interests known and asked his friends to keep an eye out for anything that looked really promising. It didn't take long for a phone call to come.

"Get on to your computer, look at this website but don't react to the name."

This had to be good. Cliff opened his laptop.

"1-800-Got-Junk."

"Oh, God." Cliff's heart sank. **Had he really fallen this far?** But as he perused the colorful website filled with pictures of guys sitting on cool-looking trucks, something clicked. Cliff could **actually** see the need for this kind of service. **After all, everybody has junk, the detritus of our consumer culture. Hot-water heaters gone cold. Computers storing nothing but dust. Disgusting mattresses. Boxes of mementos from times you no longer care to remember. A**

wood pile from back when people burned wood. All the stuff we own but hate — here was a company, staffed by reputable people, that would **make it disappear.** Customers could trust that anything that could be reused would be donated, all recyclables recycled, and all trash would be properly disposed of. His own basement could certainly benefit from the services of 1-800-Got-Junk!

Cliff dropped his superior attitude. Maybe one person's junk really was another person's treasure – *his*.

Cliff saw much more than the junk hauling business itself. He saw the potential for building a brand, and that played directly to his strengths. He knew what his role could be and knew it was the right fit. It was time to have another conversation with his wife that Cliff never expected. The former executive of a large corporation was ready to go all in on a junk collecting business. Sanford & Son on wheels. If Cliff's wife was supportive before, she was now eligible for sainthood.

But now he had to impress an even tougher audience: the 1-800-Got-Junk management team.

While the company was new to Cliff, it had already received a lot of publicity. They had been written about in the *Wall Street Journal* and *Fortune magazine.* Interest from potential franchisees was **boiling over,** which allowed Got Junk to be selective. "It was hard to even get a hold of them," Cliff told me. "I'm on the teleconference with 50 people—50 prospective franchise owners—plus their management team. And their management team is telling everybody about the company. And then after the meeting, if you were interested, you needed to get in touch with them, and then they would start the process with you."

There were two other prospective owners from Cincinnati on the call with Cliff. He wondered, "So what happens two nights from now, when there are another 50 people? How many other people from Cincinnati are going to be on the market?"

It felt like a do or die moment and he knew he had to be decisive.

When the call was finished, he walked upstairs and told his wife, "There are two other people from Cincinnati. If we don't act now, that's ok. But somebody else will."

It was junk or be junked. They made the decision right then and there: **they would do the junking.**

Cliff was **put in touch with** one of the company founders, Brian Scudamore, to get started on the **application** process. The two developed a plan and discussed budgeting before sending Cliff into a second, in-person interview in Vancouver. After the second interview, presuming that everything went well, Cliff would hand over a big check. "But it was the toughest one-day interview that I had ever been through." He would later learn that, of the 20 people in his interview class only one quarter had been accepted. **The rest were literally not good enough to haul away the trash!**

But Cliff had made it. Over the next month, he and his wife got business applications, licenses, and ordered trucks; everything they needed to bring 1-800-Got-Junk to Cincinnati.

They started small. Armed with two leased trucks and a "war room" in their basement, Cliff and his wife mapped out the entire city and planned their marketing efforts street-by-street. "It was a guerilla marketing program in the beginning," he describes, "Our trucks were very colorful and said 1-800-Got-Junk all over them. We would go to specific neighborhoods or areas, park the truck, and hang up a big banner. Then we put on these big blue clown wigs—"

I had to interrupt him. "Clown wigs? Come on."

Cliff smiled, "Clown wigs. That was me every morning. I loved it."

It's a part of the 1-800-Got-Junk culture and if someone is not willing to put on a blue wig, they are simply not a fit for the company. **(Maybe that's where IBM went wrong. Pocket squares and skinny ties are no match for a cobalt-colored Afro.)** Cliff understood that. He had to honor the philosophy and culture that helped Got Junk stand out. "We want the person who's going to say, 'Give me that wig.' Because not only will they do great marketing, which builds our brand awareness, but they'll dazzle the customer once they get there as well. When we started out, no one knew we existed so our goal was to build brand awareness. Thousands of people had to know about us today that didn't know about us yesterday, and tomorrow, thousands of people have to know about us. And that was our job. That was our mission."

If there had been any doubt that Cliff was all in on his franchise, the blue clown wig surely **scared it away.** He and his wife were 100% dedicated to running a growing, successful business and Cliff credits its success to that mentality. "We could not fail. We had nothing to fall back on." Cliff is an entrepreneur at heart and has the stomach for a higher risk profile but he appreciates the **backstop** that comes with owning a franchise. "Had I started the business that I talked about on my own, there would have been plenty of times that we wouldn't have had that structure behind it. And, if you have the right fortitude, you can still make it that way, but the nice thing about a franchise is if you pick the right one, the system is good."

The franchise system gives you the backbone, it gives you the model, and it gives you people that are there to help you. And there are plenty of times you need help, whether you're on top of the world or in the bottom of a ditch. For Cliff Brahm and his wife, the nicest thing of all was that they had the best of two worlds: the security and resources that come with being part of a larger company, and the freedom that comes with being an entrepreneur.

You're your own boss, but you have a team backing you up, kind of like LeBron James.

Tim Groves and Cliff Brahm were extremely successful businessmen who'd gone about as far as you can go inside Corporate America without actually running the place. They lived in different parts of the country, worked in entire different industries, and experienced slightly different fates. Yet they shared an overwhelming desire to call their own shots, to build something that was theirs. The franchise model made that dream a reality; it turned the possible into the actual. Its lower risk, built-in support system and proven business methods worked for these two men.

One of them cured his mid-life malaise by starting a medical business. The other hauled his frustrations away to the dump. What handy metaphor could a franchise business do for *you*? Start thinking!

CHAPTER SIX

SHOW ME THE MONEY: HOW TO FINANCE YOUR ENTREPRENEURIAL VENTURE

It takes money to make money. It doesn't matter if you're at the blackjack table, investing in **stocks**, or starting your own business. In each instance, you need money just to get in the game, and you need more money if you want to see a meaningful return on your investment. **(Although, in the case of blackjack, the less invested the better.)**

I thought about this a lot as I interviewed each of the entrepreneurs in this book. How were they doing it? When I put together those traveling plays for three summers after Star Trek was cancelled, I used savings to start but then flipped the box office receipts from each stop's week-long run to finance and produce the next week's performances. I didn't get rich off it, but the system worked, I got to act, and I supported my family.

Where were these entrepreneurs getting their money? How much did they need? How much did they actually get? The answers, like everything about these inspiring business owners, were all over the map. Thomas Betts sold his boat and the house where his children grew up to buy farmland and his first seven alpacas. Jeff Frank partnered with a silent investor to start Simplicity Sofas. Geri Brin got a loan from her sister to build the website that became FabOver50. Cliff Brahm got a small business loan from his local regional bank to buy his 1-800-GOT-JUNK franchise. Julie Cole bootstrapped Perfect Rubber Mulch on the side of her landscaping business until it got so profitable that it became her main business.

Five different businesses, five different ways to shave a cat.

You're probably saying to yourself, *'That's great, but how can **I** get the money I need to start **my** business?'* That's a fair question. Individual stories are unique and can tell you only so much about where you can go or what you can do. So I went back to Michael Grottola: the man whose story opens this book and whose new consulting business helps aspiring entrepreneurs find funding and get on their feet.

"Most startups don't fund themselves," Michael explained. "They have a grand idea and they need somebody to fund that idea."

Playing with someone else's money – what's not to love about that? Plenty, Michael cautions. "You have to expect income that is few and far between in the beginning. You have to live with spotty cash flow," he cautioned. "If you're a 40-hour a week person, don't even start." Most of you reading this book are not the 40-hour type, or you were in the first half of your lives and then realized you wanted more.

So where do you go to fund your idea or your business? There are really four **potential sources of cash:** 1) Yourself, 2) Friends and Family, 3) Investors, 4) the Banks. Each of them has its benefits. **Each has its particular drawbacks.** Understanding your needs and your tolerance for these elements will go a long way it determining what path to take.

Funding it Yourself.

The first place to look when it comes to funding your business is the mirror. Can you fund it yourself? How much of it can you fund and for how long? Should you fund it yourself considering a) the size of investment needed and/or b) the other responsibilities you have? Do you have any other options? The answers to those questions will determine to what extent you might fund this yourself and how far down the rabbit hole you go with it. But first, let's go over your self-funding options:

** A fair amount of people want to be entrepreneurs but are 40-hour types at heart. There is no shame in this, and you will find out if you are one of those people when you take the Personal Inventory checklist at the back of the book.*

Sweat Equity – No matter your financial outlook, you will always have your sweat equity. What is that? I'll let Michael tell you. "Sweat equity means working your butt off. Weekends, nights, working around the clock." Some ideas don't necessarily require a lot of money at first, they just need hard work. Julie Cole can tell you all about that with the growth of Perfect Rubber Mulch. Most ideas, though, require both money and hard work. Just ask Jeff Frank. Despite decades in the business, he wasn't able to contribute a cent to the formation of Simplicity Sofas. He brought the designs and the hard work to build the company from the ground up. His contribution was sweat equity. **By the way, don't confuse it with something that's free. We only get so many hours on this Earth.**

Bank Accounts – The essence of self-funding is pulling from your own personal bank accounts to pay your business expenses. Brian Hess used $800,000 of his own money to perfect and market his TattleTale security system. He took investors eventually, but he got the prototype built and the business off the ground with his own money. If he had failed, he would have been flat broke. **But that didn't stop him. The only alarm bell he heard was the one he invented.**

Maybe you don't have $800,000 like Brian did. Maybe you have a savings account that you created as a rainy day fund. Maybe it's your normal checking account where your current salary gets deposited. Maybe it's a 401k, an IRA, or a money market account. Whatever these accounts are, their value to you as an entrepreneur is that they hold some generally available form of cash. You may have to pay a penalty or taxes to get to it, but it has a definable cash value that you can use.

Michael Grottola has a warning for those aspiring over-50 entrepreneurs with cash in the bank and their hand on their ATM card however. "You need to research and test your market," he told me. "You can have a great idea, but the broad question is, 'Will anyone buy it?' Then the second, narrower question is, 'If they will, why would they buy it from you?'"

Answer those questions before you punch in your pin code. **Because you only get one shot to spend your life's savings.**

Credit Cards – "Some people go out on the limb for their idea and they use zero percent credit cards," Michael said as he ran me through the self-funding options. They even use their current credit cards that already carry a balance for household expenses; credit cards that are often with the same bank where they have their checking account and their mortgage. They are so confident in their idea—or so desperate for it to succeed—that when all other options **run** out they put it on **plastic, hoping their ship comes in before their bills come due.**

"It's a dangerous game, hoping," warns Michael.

Still, there are **some amazing** stories of startups that got going on maxed out credit cards. Some of them are surely apocryphal, but a number of them are real. The popular room-renting website, AirBnB, famously bootstrapped its way through its early days **on those 16 magic digits.** Andrew Warner, the founder of the entrepreneurial-focused website Mixergy.com, built his very first successful business by going back and forth with his brother opening and maxing out **a gambler's deck of** credit cards.

Those are two compelling success stories, not to be ignored. Nor should you ignore the vast sea of anonymous business failures that funded themselves on revolving credit. Tellingly, none of the entrepreneurs in this book started their businesses this way, in large part because they recognized just how risky a proposition that is. If you search "using credit cards to fund your business" in Google, the results page might as well just flash "DANGER WILL ROBINSON, DANGER!" across it.

Equity Loans – "Some people believe in their ideas so much they will take even greater risks, like taking out equity loans." This typically takes the form of a home equity loan, as Michael described it. This is especially true for aspiring business owners over 50 who more often than not are deep into a 30-year fixed mortgage and have built up a significant amount of equity to borrow against. **No one's using those other two bedrooms, anyway, right? You might as well get something out of them.**

There are two ways to do this: one is a basic home equity loan, where you borrow a lump sum against the equity you've built up in your home. This is something you might consider if your idea requires a big upfront capital infusion for equipment or materials or land to get the business off the ground. This is a path Thomas Betts could have pursued, for instance, when he purchased the land and the 7 alpacas to start his alpaca farm (he chose a different path, if you remember).

"The second way is called a Home Equity Line of Credit," Grottola explained, "or HELOC for short." A HELOC uses the same source of collateral as a normal home equity loan—the equity built up in the home—but instead of advancing the entire sum, the borrower uses it **piecemeal. Debt can be run up or paid down**, not unlike a credit card. **But interest is typically quite low, very much *unlike* a credit card.** New entrepreneurs have been known to use a HELOC for unexpected one-time expenditures, covering payroll on months when they're short, making small to mid-size improvements.

The benefit of the home equity line of credit is that it doesn't feel like you're taking on massive debt or leveraging yourself to the hilt. **The downside is that you really are – and it's a slippery slope.** It's very easy to borrow that first $5000 when you're playing with $250,000. Before you know it, though, you tack another zero onto the end of that $5000, you do it twice in 18 months, and boom you're $105k in debt. That is not a place most new businesses want to be.

Physical Assets – This is the route Thomas Betts chose to finance his alpaca operation. He looked at his assets, **measured** their value and their importance to him, and then he pulled the trigger. He sold his family home to buy farmland and a house on the other side of the Cascade Range. He sold his prized **racing yacht** to buy the first seven alpacas. **Out went the mainsails, in came the hay bales**. For a man at his wits end with the corporate grind, his decision makes all the sense in the world.

Using your physical assets to fund your company is perhaps the least risky of the other self-funding options because you are not putting yourself in hock to a bank or a credit card company. You are converting physical assets into a different type of physical asset: cash. The tricky part is to convert ***only enough*** of those assets to finance your vision, while still leaving you with a house to sleep in, a car to drive, and a few suits to wear to meetings. **Because if your dream goes up in smoke, you at least want to own an ashtray.**

As you can see, there are a number of ways to fund your idea yourself; a number of assets both tangible and intangible. But as Michael Grottola reminded me, "Thinking in advance is the most valuable asset you have. You will want to test a lot of things before you pony up your savings or go deep into debt for an idea."

Where do you test these things, though? Who do you test them on? I asked Michael both questions, out of sheer curiosity. His answer: the same group of people who can help get you off the ground if you pass muster with them.

FRIENDS & FAMILY

Your friends and family are the perfect **focus group** for judging your idea. They are removed enough from it to give you an honest, objective 3rd party opinion, but close enough to care about you and weigh how important the idea is to you. If the idea has flaws, or it's just plain bad, they will bring you back to Earth and keep your feet on the ground. If it's great and they're excited about it, they can give you just the boost you need to get your fledgling business off the ground with seed money. **And if you ever show up on their doorstep wearing nothing but a barrel, at least they won't have to ask why.**

Geri Brin went the friends and family route for seed money to start both her first business and her current one, FabOverFifty. She went to her younger sister, a very successful businesswoman. Her sister loved her ideas, told her to go for it, and cut her a check. It wasn't a lot — just enough—but it was more than a loan; it was a vote of confidence.

That is the beauty of seed money, especially when it comes from family and friends. It's validation of your idea—your passion—from people whose opinions you care about and trust, delivered in the most meaningful way possible for an entrepreneur: financial support.

But sometimes friends and family can only offer you their moral support. Cash, for any number of possible reasons, isn't **on the table. At that point — in addition to looking for some new family — you** have to look for a different class of financial backers: investors.

INVESTORS

Like the suits many of them favor, investors come in many stripes. There are angel investors who have essentially made a profession out of giving companies seed money. There are venture capitalists (VCs) who typically fund at much higher levels than seed money investments and at various stages as your company grows. And now there is crowdfunding, where you can solicit backers via social media in exchange for rewards or equity.

ANGEL INVESTORS

An angel investor is pretty much just a rich person who likes to support startups whose ideas they believe in. Just like striking out on your own and hiring yourself feels very risky, investing in someone who is going out on their own to hire themselves is also risky. That's why most angel investors ask for a lot in return for their money. Since most startups fail, they have to account for that risk, so they will ask for an amount of equity that seems out of line for the amount of money they're willing to give. **You may be a good person with a great idea, but from their perspective you're still a longshot.**

Not very *angelic*, is it? Unfortunately, **them's** the breaks when it comes to angel investing. If you don't have assets to leverage or credit to work with or friends and family who can help, angel investors are your next best bet when it comes to getting your idea up and running. And this is how the angel investing game is played. Look at it this way: it's better to have 75% of something than 100% of nothing.

VENTURE CAPITAL

Venture capital is a much bigger beast than angel investing. It involves much, much larger sums of money, many more laws and SEC regulations, and a degree of maturity as a company that many new entrepreneurs have not reached when they're still trying to figure out how to fund their idea.

You know what a *silent partner* is? Well venture-capital

firms are the opposite. They often come onboard not just as investors but as advisors. For those of you who are tired of the corporate rate race and want to be your own boss, free and clear, dealing with venture capital firms might induce some anxiety or a bit of PTSD.

After talking with Michael Grottola about venture capital, it seems pretty clear that you shouldn't worry about this path until your business plan is fully fleshed out and your idea requires a big chunk of change.

CROWDFUNDING

Crowdfunding is by far the most exciting development in the area of entrepreneurship since the invention of the Internet. Websites like Kickstarter and IndieGogo allow fledgling companies to solicit financial support from users for a variety of things—product development, product launch, equipment needs, marketing campaigns, etc.—in exchange for rewards. Sometimes that reward is a simple "thank you." Other times it's one of the first products off the assembly. Still other times it's an invitation to a VIP launch party **where crowd funders can meet the star of the show — you!**

Since Kickstarter launched in 2009, its listed projects have received over $1 billion in pledged support. The companies who list those projects are raising a ton of money in the process. The smartwatch company Pebble raised $10 million and sent its profile into the stratosphere. Pretty smart! The writers and producers of the canceled TV show "Veronica Mars" raised north of $5 million to do a movie version, **including** nearly $3m on the *first day*! Where are all the TJ Hooker and Denny Crane fans, that's what I want to know!

There are a few of things that make crowdfunding a great opportunity for over-50 entrepreneurs with a product idea. First, it allows you to raise money to build your product without having to give up equity. **(Now *that's* more like an angel!)** All you have to do is come up with cool things to give the people who have agreed to support you. Second, it gives you a giant pool of your first customers, all of whom have **conveyed that** they like what you're **doing**. Customer acquisition is one of the most difficult problems new businesses face, Michael Grottola tells me, and crowdfunding seems to have cracked that nut. Sounds good to me. Lastly, because most of the people operating on Kickstarter and IndieGogo are young, an older person with a great idea really stands out. You have a great opportunity to get attention not just from site users but from the press. **By its very nature, crowdfunding makes a very public splash for your enterprise.**

For some of you, however, raising $50,000 and getting several hundred paying customers isn't enough. Maybe you have a service business or a product that has institutional customers, or maybe you have a more sizeable funding issue. For companies like yours, the newest form of crowdfunding is opening doors that were previously guarded jealously by hedge funds and venture capital firms.

It's called equity crowdfunding. **Just like it sounds,** equity crowdfunding allows you to raise money online in exchange for **an ownership stake. If Kickstarter is for enthusiasts who want to be**

part of something new, these platforms are for real investors who want to make real money. A world of investors who were previously out of your league can now find you and decide if your plan is worth a few bucks — or a few hundred thousand.

At the top of the class are sites that do due diligence like a normal venture capital firm. They scrutinize your business plan, your financials, they examine the market you're operating in and the size of the opportunity. **It's a high bar to clear**, but if you make it, you're looking at smart, clean, reliable money that won't magically disappear or get tied up when it's time to cash the checks.

Sites like MicroVentures.com based out of Austin, Texas, run by two smart guys named Bill Clark and Tim Sullivan. Or AngelList.co based in San Francisco, run by Naval Ravikant. When Michael Grottola broke down this crowdfunding revolution for me, I was so intrigued that I went online to search for some of these sites. These were the two that kept coming up as being the most reliable with the best opportunities. If your idea is at the point where you can confidently seek investment from a crowdfunding platform, this is probably how you want to do it.

A word of warning though: At the bottom end of this young industry are sites that will post your investment opportunity with as little as a business plan and a fancy PowerPoint deck. The barrier to entry here is low, but so is the reliability and sophistication of the typical investor who commits money. **As with anything else, if a crowdfunding site seems too good to be true, it probably is.**

Of course, crowds are not known for their patience. If your idea is still in the planning and building phase, your next best bet is to actually go a more traditional route and seek funding from an institution **whose job it is to hand money out to promising businesses. Luckily, your town is full of them.**

THE BANK

It's a classic scene of terror and doubt: Walking into a bank with your hopes and dreams neatly laid out over several dozen **sheets** of paper. Sitting before a loan officer with a big rubber stamp. **Suddenly wondering if you were nuts to even think this thing up.** Fundamentally it's no different than going to any of the previous money sources we've discussed, but it turns a lot of people inside out.

Here's the thing though: a bank's ***whole job*** is to lend you money. Assuming you're qualified, of course. It's how they make money—on the interest and fees they charge. Ask any loan officer and they'll tell you that they are looking for a reason to give you the money. It's your job to present your idea in a way that gives them that reason. **So go ahead and give them one!**

Before he bought a 1-800-GOT-JUNK franchise, Cliff Brahm failed at this the first time he went to his bank for a small business loan. He had what he felt was a strong idea related to the field he had just left with a number of very talented people on board to make this idea a reality. **But here's all the bank heard: "*Junk*!" Cliff was right, of course; it was a great business idea! But his job at that moment was to make the bankers as comfortable about going into the trash business as he was.**

If you're a creditworthy applicant with a good idea and a strong business plan, a straight bank loan or a small business loan is not outside the realm of possibility. In fact, it might be your surest bet after utilizing your own physical assets. So don't let the bank intimidate you. You're on the same team: they want you to succeed as much as you do.

Once you've made the leap to becoming an entrepreneur — surely one of the scariest decisions in a person's life — the next step is almost as daunting: pulling your idea out of your head and planting it in the earth. Turning it into a real business. You owe it to yourself and your vision to consider every source possible to fund your dream.

The entrepreneurs in this book have businesses that are about as wide-ranging as you can get, but if they have anything in common **(other than their lovely salt-and-pepper hair)** it is that they pursued all possible avenues to make their dreams a reality, then chose the path that made the most sense for **them**.

You can, and should, do the same.

CHAPTER SEVEN

CATCHING UP TO GET AHEAD: TECHNOLOGY IS YOUR FRIEND NOT THE ENEMY

This book is filled with success stories about people just like you:

Michael Grottola, "right-sized" from his six-figure job on his 65th birthday, who used his engineering background, entrepreneurial spirit and retirement fund to **change his life, starting a** consulting business **that's helping others change theirs.**

Tom Betts and Dave Bateman, both **burnt out on** the corporate rate race **but not on their own prospects,** seized timely opportunities to learn new businesses and buy into them with resources they'd accumulated over the years. **Not for the faint of heart – or thin of wallet!**

Geri Brin and Julie Cole, **whose industries could not have been more different, but who both leveraged the reach of the Internet to become self-made businesswomen.**

Cliff Brahm and Tim Groves, **successful corporate executives who looked for something new and found it in the franchise model.** They're busier than ever, growing by leaps and bounds and **relishing their success – and their independence.**

Jeff Frank and Brian Hess, **who identified problems in their respective industries, invented solutions, then used the fruits of middle age – money and relationships – to turn those solutions into businesses.**

Whether they were right-sized, down-sized, burned out, **or just ready for a new adventure,** these over-50 entrepreneurs **gave themselves a second chance by** hiring themselves. I love these men and women because I see bits of my own story in each of theirs. I empathize with their fears and tough choices. I rejoice in their success the way my friends, family and fans rejoiced in my own after I reinvented myself as an artist or the Priceline guy or Denny Crane. I learn from their failures the way they learned from mine, as I discovered with great humility during our interviews.

As I sit here finishing this book in my office at home in Kentucky, surrounded by memories from my early years, my eye is repeatedly drawn to something much newer: my Google Calendar. It is packed with meeting requests, conference-call reminders, project due dates; all color-coded and time-stamped like a kaleidoscope of opportunity. What I find most striking about this is that nearly all of items on my calendar—hell, the calendar itself—are born of the choices and successes from the last 10 years, facilitated by the explosion of technology, social media and mobile devices. Things like Facebook, Twitter, YouTube, iPhones, iPads, WordPress, cell phone cameras, etc.

It's like the bridge of the *Enterprise* – and I'm a real captain this time!

Without these tools—and that's what they are, tools—my Brown Bag Wine Tasting series on YouTube wouldn't be possible. Do I make a lot of money from that? Or course not. But it's fun, it keeps me in touch with good people who I like, and it keeps me sharp in front of the camera. All of those things, when you combine them in other areas, those do make me a lot of money.

Take Twitter, for instance. You could never mount a more modest stage: you get 140 characters. Your picture's in the corner. And that's it – Twitter! And yet I have nearly two million people following my every word – can you believe it!?! With this tool I can speak directly to fans. **They** give me feedback on things like my new album or my Shatoetry app, or my appearances at Star Trek conventions. All that feedback makes me better at those things, which makes the products better, and adds value to the lives and experiences of my fans.

Think of it as 140 characters... with zero limits.

Young people understand the power of these **assets** implicitly. They take the **technology** for granted at times (welcome to young people!) because they've grown up immersed in it. In fact, those of us who **weren't raised around** this technology might argue that young people's interactions are defined by them. **(And if we're not careful we might even breathe an annoyed sigh when we say so.)** But do you know who else understands the importance of technology?

Michael and Tom and Dave and Geri and Julie and Cliff and Tim and Jeff and Brian.

Each of them recognized early in the growth of their entrepreneurial ventures that **21st century weapons** would be critical to their **survival. No,** they hadn't grown up with **social media or mobile devices;** understanding them wouldn't be second nature like it is for their children and will be for their grandchildren. But they embraced the technology anyway. They did what Sheryl Sandberg, the COO of Facebook, told a generation of professional women to do: lean into the problem. Lean into the discomfort and unfamiliarity in order to conquer it.

That choice, I discovered as I talked to people all across the country, is the only major difference between those Baby Boomers who will read this book and those who won't because they're too busy expanding their businesses or building the next phase of their lives. They've already embraced the technology and applied the same discipline and effort to learning it that they applied to raising children, fighting injustice, accumulating wealth and building our future.

Which is another way of saying: This is not a complete book. This is not the final frontier. It is still missing one thing: ***your* story.** And for the vast majority of Americans over 50 years old who are struggling in the turbulent new economy, the reason your story is not in this book is because you have not yet made this choice. That's the bad news: you have to catch yourself up.

Here is the good news: catching up is easy. **It's literally something a 2-year-old can do!**

I spoke to Ezra Firestone one last time about this. He lives in New York City, but travels all over the world talking to groups who are trying to build and grow businesses of their own. I caught up with him on the phone in an airport lounge between flights. He crystallized the issue perfectly, I think.

"The barrier to entry from a technology standpoint has gotten really low," he said, "and the Boomer generation is leveraging that new technology as well as anyone else. In fact, they're leveraging it better because they get more done in a shorter period of time."

In other words, you have a pre-Internet attention span.

Use it!

Off the top of his head, Ezra rattled off a dozen educational resources at their disposal as well as a number of online platforms that make it very easy to build businesses, many of which we've already touched on here and in previous chapters: WordPress, Shopify, Etsy, Amazon, Khan Academy, the list goes on.

As Ezra's voice cut through the chatter of the international departures lounge, it reminded me of when I first had to tackle these same technology issues well into my 70s. A website and email were easy. I could have someone build and manage those things for me, and that's what I've done for several years. But all this other technology, if it was going to be effective for my brand and my business, I would actually have to learn how it worked and how to use it. No one was going to beam me up to the ship – I had to get there on my own.

I struggled at first, especially with Twitter -- 140 characters? Have you not seen me on the stage or heard me tell a story? You cannot tie this stallion to so short a rope! That's how I felt at the beginning. Then my assistant Kathleen found these two gentlemen who ran a small service called "Catch Me Up" that was designed for people just like me. They'd just made their second video about Twitter and she forwarded it to me. It was a revelation. It answered all the simple questions I felt too silly or stupid asking. In a lot of ways, I credit learning how to use Twitter properly as the reason I've been able to build the following I currently enjoy.

The Internet is not the Field of Dreams. It's not "build it and they will come," as Julie Cole so aptly put it. You have to use the technology **to give people** something that they want. **That's a lot easier said**

than done, but if you pull it off on a regular basis, these technological innovations can unlock business success no matter the field, the product, **or the service** (I learned that from "Catch Me Up" as well).

And there isn't just one way to learn about this stuff. There are countless tools at your disposal—as both Ezra and I can attest. **But there's one ingredient no one else can provide: You.** If you don't make the choice to join the ranks of the over-50 entrepreneurs in this book who hired themselves - **the choice** to get caught up -
then you never will.

When the boarding announcement for Ezra's flight home came through the loudspeaker in the lounge, I quickly thanked him for his insight so he could get packed up and on his way. But before he did, he left me with a pearl of wisdom that I want to leave with you:

"American baby boomers are a generation of people who reinvented every decade of their lives. They're not sitting on the porch in their 50s and 60s. They're not lying in bed in their 70s, waiting to die. They're out there doing things. They're learning to snowboard, they're learning to ski, and they're becoming yoga instructors and building businesses."

Ezra paused to take a breath, or maybe for effect (watch his videos - he's very good), before concluding his point by addressing me directly:

"They're not afraid of technology, Bill. It's just new and it's different and it's not what they grew up with. But what I'm seeing is that they're getting out there and doing it, and they're doing it well." Amen.

Take these stories to heart, listen to experts like Ezra, and learn from my trials and triumphs. And if you do only one thing after you close the cover on this book, please just get yourself caught up. It will put the next phase of your life into warp drive.

Plus, you'll finally know what your kids are talking about! If you *want* to, that is.

APPENDIX

THE "CATCH ME UP" PERSONAL INVENTORY CHECKLIST

This book is full of stories about people just like you. People who looked at the second half of their lives and didn't just ask for more; they made something better. But they didn't start from square one. (Who even remembers square one?) They used everything they'd gained in the first half of their lives to make that dream a reality. The first step for each of them, whether they knew it at the time or not, was to take a personal inventory. Michael did it, Geri did it, Jeff did it, I did it, we all did it. So should you.

This checklist is designed to make that inventory easy and useful. It is made up of all the questions our over-50 entrepreneurs asked and answered as they prepared to hire themselves.

SECTION ONE:

WHAT I HAVE

This section covers everything you have going for you. Most people do not realize how much they are working with. Answering these questions will clarify the assets you have at your disposal as you decide what to do next.

1. WHAT AM I GOOD AT?

(ex. Finances, communicating, reading people, computers, etc.)

____

____

2A. AM I AN EXPERT IN ANYTHING I AM GOOD AT?

(ex. Finances, communicating, reading people, computers, etc.)

____

____

b) Of those areas of expertise, which general skill type do they most closely fall into: Making, Selling, Teaching?

____

3A. WHAT AM I PASSIONATE ABOUT?

____

____

b) What drives me? (if I don't believe in "passion")

____

4A. WHAT ASSETS DO I HAVE?

(ex. Stocks, home, land, savings, etc.)

____

____

b) What is their functional, net value (minus taxes & fees) if I sold them?

____

5. WHAT IS THE SHAPE OF MY NETWORK?

(ex. Who do I know? What do they do? How could they help me?)

NAME:	EXPERTISE:	AREA THEY COULD HELP:
________	________	________
________	________	________
________	________	________

NAME:	EXPERTISE:	AREA THEY COULD HELP:

SECTION TWO:
WHAT I NEED

This section covers everything you require. These are the non-negotiable, must-haves. There are any number of inspirational books and motivational speakers out there who will tell you that life is too short for doubts and second-guessing. They will tell you that all you need to do is find your passion and damn the torpedoes, full speed ahead! Sorry, but that's idiotic. Most of us have families to support, commitments to fulfill, responsibilities to meet. These do not all carry equal weight, but each requires consideration appropriate to its importance in your life. The more important, the more of a need it is to be filled. Understanding what your needs are helps determine the scope of what is possible.

1. WHAT DO I ABSOLUTELY NEED TO BE HAPPY OR COMFORTABLE?

Rank them. (ex. Financial security, family, a job you love, fellowship, etc)

NEEDS: **RANK**

______________________________________ ________

______________________________________ ________

NEEDS: **RANK**

2. WHO IS COUNTING ON ME AND FOR WHAT?

(ex. Raising grandchildren, disabled friend, deacon in your church, volunteer fire department)

3. WHAT KIND, AND HOW MUCH, OF A LIMITING FACTOR DO THESE COMMITMENTS PRESENT?

(ex. $5000 monthly financial outlay, 23 hours a week of my time, I have to stay 50 miles from home, etc.)

____

____

____

____

____

4. HOW MUCH MONEY DO I NEED TO LIVE THE SECOND HALF OF MY LIFE THE WAY I WANT?

(ex. Per year, per month, etc.)

____

____

____

____

SECTION THREE:
WHAT I WANT

Now for a little "you time." We've covered what you have and what you need, this section is about what you want. Goals, dreams, plans—call them what you will, these are the questions to help you figure out exactly what target you should shoot for. This is no time for modesty or denial. The answers you arrive could be the most powerful motivating force in the next part of your life.

1. WHAT DO I WANT MORE THAN ANY OTHER?

(ex. To be rich, to be my own boss, a new career I love, to spend time with family, etc.)

____

____

2. HOW IMPORTANT IS MONEY TO ME? HOW MUCH DO I WANT TO MAKE?

(ex. I want to be rich, be comfortable, I don't care about money, etc.)

____

____

3. WHAT IS MY RISK TOLERANCE? WHAT AM I WILLING TO DO TO MAKE THIS HAPPEN?

(ex. Move, quit current job, sell/mortgage home, etc.)

____

____

____

____

4. DO I WANT THIS TO BE A SIDE-JOB, A CAREER, A HOBBY THAT EARNS MONEY?

____

____

____

____

CON GRAT ULAT IONS!

YOU HAVE JUST COMPLETED CATCH ME UP'S ENTREPRENEURIAL PERSONAL INVENTORY. YOUR ANSWERS TO THESE QUESTIONS SHOULD HELP YOU UNDERSTAND, AT A GLANCE, WHAT YOU ACTUALLY WANT AND WHAT YOU ARE WILLING TO DO TO MAKE IT HAPPEN. THEY SHOULD CLARIFY THE RESPONSIBILITIES AND COMMITMENTS THAT DEFINE THE BOUNDARIES OF YOUR WORLD, AS WELL AS THE NEEDS YOU MUST MEET TO FEEL COMFORTABLE WITH YOUR DECISION. **THEY SHOULD ALSO EMBOLDEN YOU WITH A GREATER APPRECIATION FOR EVERYTHING YOU HAVE GOING FOR YOU: ASSETS, SKILLS, NETWORK, EXPERIENCE AND EXPERTISE.** DO YOU ALREADY HAVE A DREAM, A PASSION, AN OPPORTUNITY? VET IT AGAINST YOUR PERSONAL INVENTORY AND PREPARE TO TAKE THE NEXT STEP WITH CONFIDENCE.

GOOD LUCK!

NOW, BOLDLY GO WHERE YOU HAVE NEVER GONE BEFORE!

AFTERWORD

Reengage and stay relevant. That is what William Shatner's new book, Catch Me Up, is all about—a collection of stories and memoirs that will inspire the folks over 50 that their best days are NOT behind them...That the future is bright!

The more we shared this message, the more we realized that this idea—the overall notion of reengagement, fostering inspiration, and how to make it a reality—was so necessary and lacking in today's day and age. How is it that something like this doesn't already exist? That's when we decided to take this idea and dive into the scary and uncertain world of crowd funding.

Prior to writing Catch Me Up, Shatner's assessment of Kickstarter was that it was essentially just a fancy way of holding out a hand to ask for money. After going through this experience, it's safe to say that Kickstarter is much more than that.

To him, it was market valuation: Does the world want this?

It was social proof: Does the world need this?

It was demographic research: Who is our target and secondary audience?

After exceeding our funding goal by 120%, we can safely say that people do want this. After receiving the outpouring of support from both young and...not-so-young...it was clear that people need this. But that last question perhaps yielded the most interesting finding.

We were initially under the impression that our core demographic would be the children of the baby boomers; those who are growing ever more impatient with their parents' "older ways."

We were wrong. We found that our core constituency was the well over 50 set. There was an intense desire among the over 50's to improve and enrich their lives by being their own bosses. There was a dormant spirit of entrepreneurship that only started to emerge with the bad experiences in their professional lives. They wanted to take their fates into their own hands...they wanted to be their own boss.

That's when Kickstarter grew into more than a book. We want the CMU website to serve as the means to teach at a slower pace and with easy-to-follow terminology. We will build a community of like-minded entrepreneurs in their older years and support one another. We will help each other continue to stay relevant.

CATCH ME UP IS A MOVEMENT.

Looking back at the inception of the Kickstarter campaign art and page design, we made conscious decisions on everything that we wrote, designed, and framed for the page.

We started with the logo. Before we could begin visualizing the logo, we needed to identify the goal. It should be hopeful, honorable, professional, stable...something that can be relied on. We went through vigorous research on color theory and the emotions that certain colors can exude. The logo you see in front of you today is the result of hours and hours of identity and research.

It was truly a labor of love for and by William Shatner, and he made sure that every decision we made on our Kickstarter page was backed by research and reason.

Even our promotions and social media pushes were well thought out well (well well) in advance.

WOM - Word of Mouth. Shatner and our team shared our Kickstarter with friends, family, and the press.

Press Releases - We also applied a more traditional approach to the way we were promoting the campaign by sending out a Press Release. We were thrilled with the success of the press pickup.

CBC - http://bit.ly/1FtmOh3

Business Journal - http://bit.ly/1Cp8KWp

The Street - http://prn.to/1EkWOAb

NBC - http://bit.ly/1EkWSQo

ABC - http://bit.ly/18zbxyE

CNN - http://cnn.it/1LkB3JR

Facebook Ads: We launched several campaigns targeting specific audiences. We broke our paid promotions down by four different campaign groups: Pre-Launch, Live, Going Strong, & Final Stretch.

1. The pre-launch campaign was simply about creat ing hype and building awareness.

2. The live campaign was to let people know they could finally back and join our mission to re-inspire baby boomers across the US.

3. The Going Strong campaign's purpose was to keep CMU relevant and in front of the eyes of our back ers and potential new backers.

4. The Final Stretch campaign would be our last push to get backers with a sense of urgency.

We were successfully funded after the 2nd campaign, so the last two campaigns shifted to focus on extreme gratification and thanks. Here are some example ads:

Facebook Image Ads:

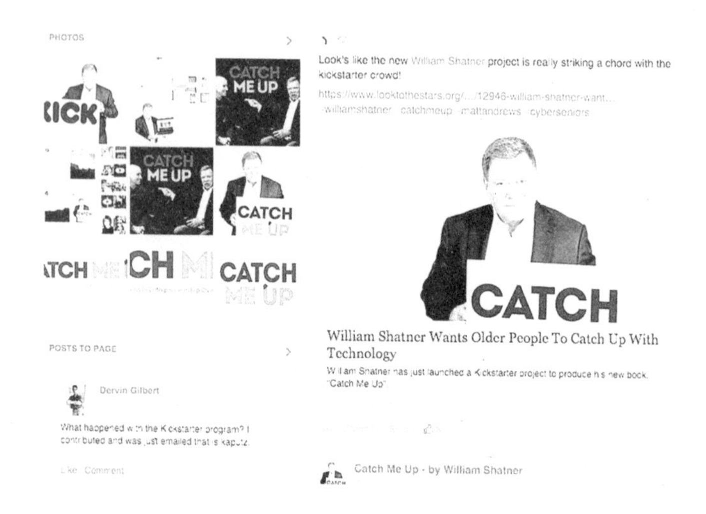

Facebook Video Ads:

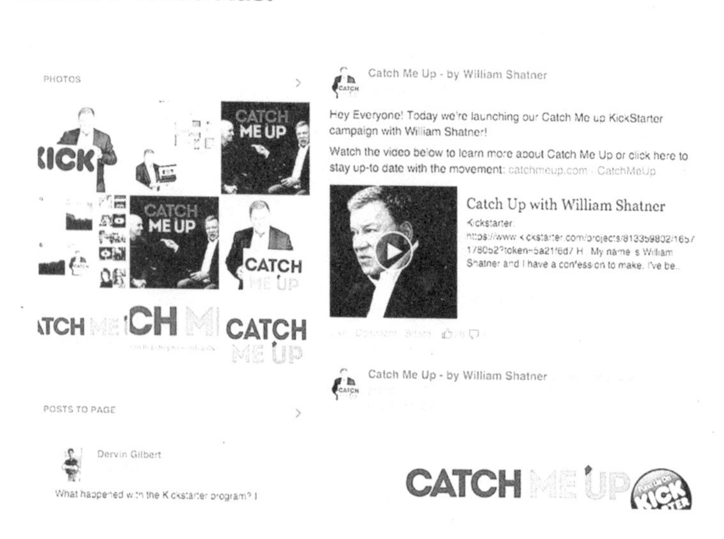

See here for a full social media plan: http://bit.ly/1Hy3LkS

Despite having many roadblocks and a limited budget, we managed to successfully fund our Kickstarter and even exceeded our goal of $50k in funding. We ended up with $60k in funding from over a thousand backers.

Now we are embarking on this movement that we were so hoping would come into fruition. We thank you for buying this book and helping us embark on our movement, where we will reengage those who have lost their way; where we will catch you up and keep you relevant; where we plan to redefine what it means to be a senior. The best days are not behind you. The future is bright.

Thank you again from the bottom of our hearts.

Most Sincerely,
The CMU Kickstarter Team